IDEAS ARRANGEMENTS EFFECTS

Systems Design and Social Justice

By Design Studio for Social Intervention

Written by Design Studio for Social Intervention
Lori Lobenstine, Kenneth Bailey and Ayako Maruyama

Design and Layout with Lois Harada
Illustrations with Ayako Maruyama and Jeffrey Yoo Warren
Cover art by Judith Leemann
Much Gratitude to Matt Hern

ISBN 978-1-57027-368-1

Released by Minor Compositions 2020
Colchester / New York / Port Watson

Minor Compositions is a series of interventions & provocations
drawing from autonomous politics, avant-garde aesthetics, and the
revolutions of everyday life.

Minor Compositions is an imprint of Autonomedia
www.minorcompositions.info | minorcompositions@gmail.com

Distributed by Autonomedia
PO Box 568 Williamsburgh Station
Brooklyn, NY 11211

www.autonomedia.org
info@autonomedia.org

Table of Contents

FOREWORD

By Arturo Escobar

I am very happy and honored to have been asked to write the Foreword to this important and unique book. I am happy because it gives me the opportunity to convey my intellectual and political enthusiasm and excitement for the vision, framework, and tools for design-driven social transformation perspective crafted by the Design Studio for Social Intervention. As I will explain shortly, I believe this book is unique in many ways; this is what makes it hugely important.

The uniqueness and originality of the book stem from the apparent simplicity of its central formula—that "Ideas are embedded within arrangements, which in turn produce effects"—coupled with two other factors; the first is the amazing degree of complexity this formula enables its authors—and all of us, in reading it—to unfold. Complexity about what? About what possibly constitutes the highest stakes of all, namely, social reality itself, or what the authors call "the social." Second, the fact that rather than this complexity leading to paralysis or a sense of defeatism about the seemingly insurmountable problems that leak from all aspects of social life, the analysis delivers with incomparable lucidity a palpable sense of the kinds of actions and strategies needed to address many of these problems and, in so doing, most fundamentally, fulfill the larger goal of "rearranging the social."

The I-A-E triplet is much more than a formula; it is a sophisticated theory of how reality gets to be what it is, and concomitantly a powerful explanation of how we have gotten stuck with profoundly oppressive and exploitative social orders. It is tempting to see older categories of social theory embedded in IAE, dressed in a new garb, such as the triplet "ideologies/structures/domination." But this would imply remaining within the realm of Big Ideas, in the face of which activists and intellectuals committed to progressive social change often feel disempowered, finding themselves at a loss regarding how to effectively transform them. Surely also the IAE framework is indebted to various critical academic trends, such as phenomenology (in its emphasis on place-making); theories of domination in terms of race, gender, class, and sexuality; systems theories and notions of self-organization, complexity and emergence; and poststructuralism (in its attention to the role of knowledge, categories and discourses in effecting particularly damaging arrangements); whatever it has borrowed from these often abstruse theories, however, it has been thoroughly reprocessed and re-woven into an original conceptualization.

Still on an academic vein, the notion of "arrangements" points at a certain kinship between the IAE framing and recent theories of assemblages; the latter have no doubt shed new understanding on how the social is the result of complex interrelations among disparate human and nonhuman elements that may acquire, over time and often at great cost, a greater or lesser degree of stability and sturdiness. However, I often find in the diverse approaches going on under the rubric of assemblages a lingering standard

geometry of entities, nodes and interconnections, and a vague
notion of politics. I would argue that the IAE proposal eludes these
problems since, in staying closer to the fluidity of social life, it
arrives at a more profoundly *relational* vision which thus grounds
a radical, yet eminently practicable, notion of politics. Moreover,
in highlighting the fact that common people and activists are
sophisticated knowledge producers and designers in their own right,
the IAE vision takes distance from academic theorizing as usual. This
by itself renders it into a transformative politics of social change.

In the pages that follow, the reader will therefore find a sophisticated
intellectual and theoretical vision, as persuasive as any fashionable
contemporary academic trend, if not more. Let me now attempt to
situate this work within the landscape of design. The book, first of all,
is a social action-oriented design theory; it offers a compelling view
of social intervention as a critical design praxis. As the authors put it,
"We believe the IAE framework can both deepen our understanding of
the social contexts we hope to change and improve, as well as expand
our capacity for designing the world we truly want." This premise
places DS4SI in conversation with the widening field of innovative
design approaches that have become salient particularly over the
past decade. The most well-known inhabitants of this field include
design for social innovation; the decolonization of design (fostered
by Afrodescendant, Indigenous, and Latina/o design theorists and
activists, such as Dori Tunstall at the Ontario Institute for Studies
in Education, OCAD, in Toronto); transition design; just design and

design justice; decolonial design; and designs from the South. As with the case of assemblage theories in the academic domain, there is a particular closeness between the notions of design for social intervention and the expanding field of social innovation design. Design for social innovation theorists such as Mariana Amatullo and Andrew Shea at Parsons School of Design, and Ezio Manzini, have pointed out at the emergent character of design as a collective practice concerned with the creation of the very conditions of social life. There is a hopeful convergence between the two frameworks; nevertheless, I feel that the IAE vision, as explained in this work, most clearly succeeds in providing us with a framework that articulates a *radical sense of politics* with a *practicable set of concept-tools* for enacting such politics in concrete settings; this is an extremely hard goal to accomplish for any framework aimed at some transformation, let alone one centered on design. Herein lies another source of uniqueness characterizing the book you are about to read.

One might restate the underlying contention of the DS4SI book framework as follows: From the Planet to the neighborhood, from nations to communities, and from households to individual persons, we are facing a social and ecological emergency, the result of long-standing and naturalized power-driven arrangements that have become pervasive in all domains of social life. Hence, it is imperative that we become attuned to the task of redesigning the social, and the key to it is to relearn to look at the complex arrangements in which the broad injuries of discrimination and systems of domination are embedded (the Big Ideas, such as racism, heterosexism, classism, and neoliberal capitalism and modernity). We may do this by taking the effects of such systems in everyday life as an entry point into a collective inquiry and a design praxis that, rather than re-inscribing or entrenching even more the same arrangements, unsettle them, fostering significant rearrangements of the social towards convivial modes of sociality, far from those mandated by corporations and the State. We no longer need to feel that lasting social change requires the wholesale overthrow of structures of domination, were this even to be possible, but that it may lie in the recurrent and iterative rearranging of the social through a renovated praxis of design. This demands from us developing the capacity to understand and sense, even "sniff out," those arrangements where forms of naturalized power are busy at work.

To be sure, we are not talking about a linear, cause-effect connection between ideas, arrangements, and effects. Rather, there are loops and twists of all kinds between them. Yet the authors give us ample clues for dealing with this intricacy of the social. A key element is contained in the principle that "effects don't naturally send us to inspecting arrangements." Racism is a case in point; confronted with the myriad instances of racial discrimination in daily life (racism's "effects"), we most often than not jump to the Big Idea ("Racism"), missing altogether the crucial domain of the arrangements that serve as relays between the big "isms" and their mundane but at times lethal effects. It is here that the DS4SI designerly imagination is best at work: in helping us see the multiple and often subtle mediations, the smaller ideas and practices that harbor the petty, but insidious, daily forms of discrimination, from schools to the media, from beliefs to infrastructures, and from government routine procedures to the enduring practices of the economy. Most importantly, it does it at the same time that it provides us with tools to imagine, and get a handle on, the kinds of changes we can most effectively pursue.

Along the way, we find incredibly insightful ideas, such as the fact that arrangements are not only designed, but designing –we are arranged by the arrangements in which we participate and even help keep in place; that effects are emergent properties of overlapping and diverse arrangements; that when reacting to social problems in our midst we often blame people while we should be scrutinizing arrangements instead; that by missing the level of arrangements in our struggle for social justice we find it hard to impact the social, while capitalism happily goes on arranging our lives; and that in questioning arrangements we need to reassess our own arrangements—the manifold ways in which we, too, are arranged—with the goal of preparing us for more explicit forms of transformative collective action. This is what social intervention is all about, and design is central to it.

Throughout their work, DS4SI strives to enact the principle that design is not just about problem-solving within existing paradigms and social orders, it is about world building, about imagining and constructing new territories of life and difference. Design for social intervention, as the authors put it, is about resetting problems in ways that contribute to rearranging the social. This principle resituates one of contemporary design's most audacious propositions—that everybody designs—squarely within the domain of social justice work. "We believe it's essential," the authors state, "for people who care about social justice to see themselves as designers of everyday life." This belief can actually be taken as the basis for a community's autonomy. As they conclude, "we use social interventions as signals, suggestions and invitations to galvanize others into this work of rearranging and changing ideas and relations." This is design's imagination at its best, the grounds for a genuinely transformative design praxis. It is a route to disclosing new worlds and bringing them into existence.

To conclude, I would say that this book "downloads" the insights of contemporary social theory, critical design debates, and activist knowledges onto the domain of daily life in extraordinarily insightful and enabling ways. It does so while embracing a politics that I would call anti-systemic, where actions have at least the potential to become dysfunctional to the Big "-isms" while simultaneously contributing to enact alternative worlds. "We need to think with the audacity of world builders," they claim in their "Letter to Our Readers." Let's heed this call with all our hearts and minds, so as to give collective form and impetus to our deepest yearnings for other worlds and worlds otherwise.

My hope is that this book-manual will be widely read and utilized in design and social justice work of all kinds. Undergraduate students will find it exceptionally helpful in reorienting their own life and professional projects towards social change agendas with a more acute sense of how their actions might contribute to enduring transformations towards socially just and ecologically mindful worlds. Even aware as I am of the fact that, whereas hundreds of books are translated every year from English into many other languages, only a trickle flow in the opposite direction, I do hope this little big book is translated into many languages worldwide. I'd like to see it in Spanish, Portuguese and French for Latin America and the Caribbean, but also in Kiswahili, Wolof, Yoruba, Urdu, Hindi, Arabic, Chinese, Mayan, Quechua and Aymara, and many other languages spoken by the peoples of the Global South. Offered in the spirit of an open access work, activists and everyday designers in these parts of the world could creatively adapt and, indeed, rewrite this work in ways appropriate to their own task of rearranging the social. Because we are all, albeit differentially, immersed in the social and ecological crisis engulfing the Planet, we need all the contributions we can gather for the urgent task of transitioning to an Earth-wise, just, and life-enhancing pluriverse of social life. Rearranging the social at myriad and diverse places and locations worldwide is a key to this most vital goal.

Arturo Escobar
Author, *Designs for the Pluriverse: Radical Interdependence, Autonomy, and the Making of Worlds*

INTRODUCTION
A Letter to our Readers

Dear Friends,

We are writing to you directly because we feel that there are many ways that our collective work towards social justice — whether it's within the nonprofit sector, the "art world," our local communities, city government, etc. — has been arranged into boxes that limit our ability to create the large scale effects that we are fighting for. To put it more concretely, while we are busy fighting oppression (often one conference, policy, protest or class at a time), our cousin or neighbor or stranger sitting next to us on the bus has no idea. We are fighting hard for social justice, but we are not very good at impacting the larger social container of everyday life. If that neighbor or cousin or stranger wanted to shape their weekend or imagine their future — how would they pick us?

Right now the actors of free market capitalism are the ones who make the shapes and forms of social life, and we as activists and artists are at best in the business of correction on a case by case basis. We think this view of ourselves and our needed reach is too limited. It cedes too much to Silicon Valley and Hollywood, which have no problem seeing themselves as the makers of tomorrow. These highly resourced, networked and even cloaked institutions are positing and building a world which includes the end of work, synthetic biology, artificial intelligence, and space travel after we've consumed the Earth's resources. It's clear that even playing tough defense is not going to get us where we need to go.

So where do we start?

We start by inviting you, our reader and ally, to see yourself as a world builder. Too often, we limit ourselves to reacting to the constant crises of the world as it is. Here at DS4SI, we believe that those of us who care deeply about social justice need to proactively see ourselves as creators of the world that we are fighting for. We believe that rearranging the social is a powerful tool for this. (We use "the social" to point to how the terms of social life are constantly being enacted and practiced, how our collective experiences are both historically based and always changing.) By taking on this re-arranging, we can bring our ideas about justice beyond the scale of our silos and into the daily lives of millions of people.

So how do we "rearrange the social"? This book begins with the premise that ideas are embedded in social arrangements, which in turn produce effects. **Part One** digs into the complexities of these ideas, arrangements and effects, and their not always linear relationships with each other. It challenges the way we too often get stuck in fighting negative effects, and spells out some of the ways that we get caught up in either blaming or arranging each other. **Part Two** makes the case that arrangements are a rich terrain for social intervention and world building. It looks at how we can create change by sensing, intervening in, and imagining new arrangements, including examples from our own work and others. **Part Three** is a bit more of a how-to: sharing tools and tricks that we use to design, test and evaluate our social interventions, as well as ways that social interventions can invite the larger public into imagining and creating a more just and vibrant world.

Hopefully this "I-A-E" framework will help you uncover new insights into your own work, as it did for us. We invite you to engage with this book in whatever way works best for you—jump around, look at the pictures, fill in the blanks, start at the back, write in the margins... Wherever you want to start, think small and think big. Question the small arrangements that shape everyday life. Imagine big arrangements and the impact we could have. What profound re-arrangement are you yearning for? We hope this book helps you find it and bring it to life!

cheers,
DS4SI

part one

BREAKING DOWN

IDEAS ARRANGEMENTS EFFECTS

Ideas-Arrangements-Effects (I-A-E) is an emergent framework, one that we have slowly come to understand and articulate. We didn't start with this; it became evident to us only as we were seeking ways to make our thinking more transparent and applicable. I-A-E is a lens that gives us a language for doing our work, but also a way to articulate what we have always been doing, long before we knew how to fully explain it. We believe sharing this framework can be a useful and coherent way to share DS4SI's thinking and work, as well as to invite others into exploring our approach.

Ideas are embedded within social arrangements, which in turn produce effects. One simple way to explain this premise is in the arrangement of chairs in a classroom. When we see chairs in straight rows facing forward, we believe the teacher is the head of the class and that knowledge flows in one direction—from the teacher to the students. In response to this, many workshop facilitators and adult-ed teachers rearrange the chairs into a circle, with the idea being that knowledge is distributed across the participants and could emerge from any place within the circle. The rows are one expression of ideas about how learning happens; the circle is another. The effects that rows or circles of chairs have on learning are important, but they are not the point here. *The point is that the arrangement produces effects.*

IDEAS

are embedded within

ARRANGEMENTS

which, in turn produce

EFFECTS

When we scan out from the common example of chairs in the classroom to the complex social arrangements of everyday life, the principle still stands: Ideas-Arrangements-Effects. They just get more intermingled and complicated. For example, arrangements like "work" flow from a myriad of ideas—weaving together ideas about value, labor, capitalism, citizenship, gender, etc. Effects of our current arrangement of "work" range from unemployment to burnout, from poverty to immigrant-bashing, from anxiety to loneliness, etc. As activists, we often attend to the effects because they are urgent—fighting for an increased minimum wage to decrease poverty, for example. As social justice practitioners, we also think a lot about the ideas that often lead to negative effects—like how racism or sexism influences who gets the higher paid positions (or even who gets hired). But the underlying arrangement of "work" is often taken for granted.

To compound this, effects don't naturally send us to inspecting arrangements. They send us back to other similar acute experiences, rather than the distributed elements of arrangements. And if we do think about arrangements, they can seem daunting.

The rearranging of chairs is much easier to do than rearranging our conceptions of time, sociality, or other institutions that glue daily life together and give shape to our collective experiences. To make things more challenging, the older and more codified the arrangement, the more it falls from the capacity to be perceived, let alone changed. These larger, sturdier social arrangements move into the realm of social permanence. For example, cars. We might argue for safer cars, greener cars, fewer cars or driverless cars, but do we ever ask the question, "Are cars as a social arrangement still beneficial? And if not, how do we proceed?"

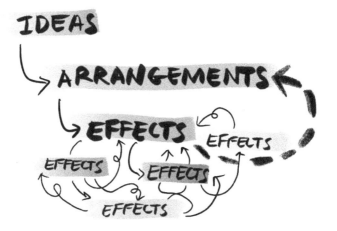

IDEAS

ARRANGEMENTS

EFFECTS

EFFECTS

EFFECTS

EFFECTS

EFFECTS

EFFECTS don't naturally send us to inspecting ARRANGEMENTS...

We believe that the IAE framework can both *deepen our understanding* of the social contexts we hope to change and improve, as well as *expand our capacity* for designing the world we truly want.

To begin, we will share some insights we've developed about each part of the IAE framework—ideas, arrangements and effects—and then lessons we've learned for how the parts relate to each other and interact.

IDEAS

1. Ideas are big and sturdy.

2. Ideas are small and tricky.

ARRANGEMENTS

1. Arrangements are hard.

2. Arrangements are soft.

EFFECTS

1. Effects are the big things we're always fighting against.

2. Effects are the little things we experience everyday.

IDEAS

Many times as humans attempt to create change,
we go back to the ideas behind the injustices we are
trying to address. Whether those ideas are notions of
democracy, justice or race, we often get trapped in
familiar discourses—complete with familiar arguments
and even familiar positions and postures. (For example
when conversations about democracy get limited
to Democrats and Republicans, or debates about
education revolve around school budgets.) We argue
heatedly and repeatedly about the big ideas, and we
get trapped there without inspecting smaller ideas and
what opportunities for change they could open up. The
discourse itself becomes a trap. It rehearses itself and
normalizes itself and ossifies the conversation, falling
into well-worn grooves. It ceases to have rigorous
curiosity, because to vary off the beaten conversation
feels dangerous or odd. We want to look at ideas
both big and small, both well inspected and largely
uninspected, as we think about how they relate to
arrangements and effects.

1) Ideas are big and sturdy.

Oftentimes we jump right from unjust effects
(achievement gap, gentrification, police violence,
poverty, etc.) back to the big ideas that repeatedly
produce them—ideas like racism, classism,
homophobia and sexism. Big ideas aren't limited to the
"isms" of course; they also include long-held notions
about freedom, progress, the American Dream, private
property, gender, democracy, and many more.

Big ideas remain sturdy because of how they embed themselves in everyday life. This used to be more obvious than it often is today. For example, racist ideas in the 17th century were explicit in institutions like slavery, and then just as obvious in the later public infrastructures of "white" and "colored" water fountains and whites-only bathrooms in the South. While we no longer have slavery or whites-only bathrooms today, we clearly have racism raising its sturdy head in countless ways. In addition, we have examples of other isms directly embedded in current arrangements today, such as transphobia and the renewed ban on transgender people in the military, or adultism and the age limit on voting.

We need to name isms when we recognize them, and we need to listen to others who recognize them when we do not. Using the IAE frame can also increase our repertoire for recognizing them as they embed themselves in the arrangements and smaller, trickier ideas shaping what we call everyday life.

The ubiquitous "white" and "colored" water fountains of the past have been removed, but the countless ways that blacks are targeted while doing daily things like driving, shopping or resting show that racism continues to be a sturdy idea.

2) Ideas are small and tricky.

We deploy (and hide) our big ideas by embedding them in our beliefs about daily life—they become whitewashed, so to speak, as more "innocent" values, beliefs and ways of life. They fall from the realm of critique and dialogue and into the realm of expectations and assumptions.

A few examples of these "innocent" ideas include:

- How to dress (or eat, or speak) "appropriately"
- Who should be listened to, believed or trusted
- How big your body should be or how loud your voice should be
- What healthy food is, what good food is, or what food you should (and shouldn't!) bring for lunch
- Who the audience is for public life and culture
- What and who is attractive
- What qualifies someone for a job
- What makes a neighborhood "safe" or "dangerous"

We know how to call out racism, but do we know how to intervene in "appropriate" or "trusted" or "welcome"? When the whites-only water fountain gets replaced by the whites-mostly coffee shop or beer garden, we only know how to point it out when a black person is explicitly treated unfairly. We don't frequently challenge the numerous tricky ideas (consumerism, aesthetics, etc.) that white-wash those spaces in the first place.

The clearer we get on the specifics of the coming together of arrangements and the ideas embedded within those arrangements, the more ideas we might have for creating change, and the more site-specific and useful points of leverage we might find. We need to get better at understanding how big ideas have become ingrained in the operating system of everyday life—how something as seemingly innocent as being a fan of a major sports team (complete with its jerseys, rituals, parades, stadium, etc.) can stand in for tribal whiteness and manliness. When we can find the more subtle and tricky ideas expressed in the workings of our lives, we get better grips on the kinds of changes we can make.

How sturdy ideas like racism get embedded
in tricky ideas like...

ARRANGEMENTS

Arrangements give shape to our shared experience. They are all around us, at all sorts of scales, overlapping, creating both order and chaos as they flow over us and under our consciousness. Arrangements include the football season with its schedules, stadiums, and fantasy leagues; the highway with its cars (with and without drivers!), speed limits, and exits; the grocery store with its rows and stacks, prices, and cash registers; Christmas with its work holidays, shopping and wrapping gifts, and assumptions of Christianity; the 9-5 day, the police, and the list goes on. We tend to participate in the arranged because it is our shared social container. And for the most part we simply take it for granted. This is one reason we at DS4SI pay so much attention to arrangements! **They are a rich and frequently overlooked terrain for creating change.**

We can talk about arrangements as "how the chairs are arranged in the room," which is what we call a "hard" or physical arrangement. We also talk about the chair itself as an arrangement for learning, as something that conveys that bodies should be passive while they learn. When we overlap that with how students are supposed to listen to their teachers or raise their hands before speaking, we start to point at what we call "soft" arrangements—which can be even sturdier than the chairs themselves, but harder to point to!

What soft and hard arrangements can you point to?

1) Arrangements are hard.

We have the architectural and industrial arrangements of built things like desks, buses and cities. These are the easiest to point to, but in some cases the hardest to re-arrange (depending on scale). It is a lot easier to re-arrange chairs than to re-arrange a built environment. Hard arrangements range in scale from the toilet, chair or bed, to airports, strip malls and industrial farms.

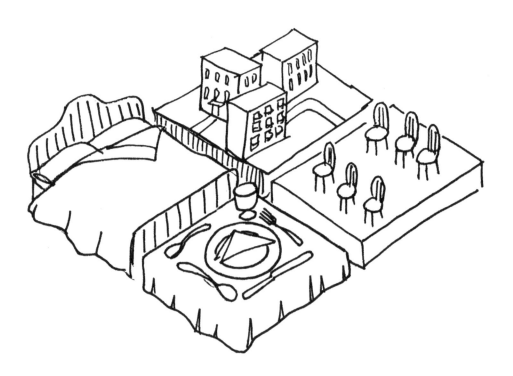

We explored the hard arrangement of the kitchen in our intervention Public Kitchen (p.98). We wanted to point to how many elements of our daily lives flowed from the assumption that everyone had a private home with its own kitchen. We wanted to explore how daily life could be more convivial and affordable if we had an arrangement like a Public Kitchen. We began with the question: If we had public kitchens—like public libraries—how would it change social life? What other arrangements—both hard and soft—would grow out of such an infrastructure?

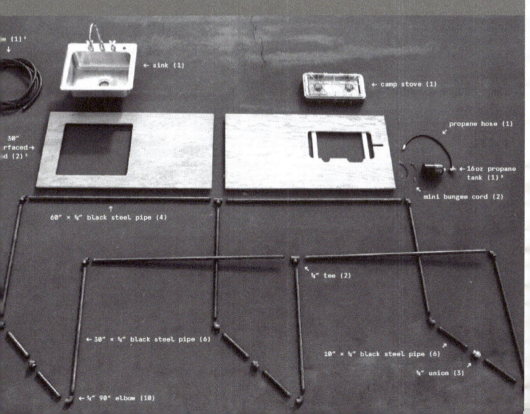

2) Arrangements are soft.

Soft arrangements are the less tangible arrangements—how routines, expectations, and long-held assumptions shape the everyday. They include routines like how the day is punctuated by breakfast, lunch, and dinner, or arrangements that put "girls" and "boys" on different sports teams or in different bathrooms, or that there is a such thing as normal or deviant, and we create arrangements like jail for the deviant. A relatively new set of arrangements have cropped up on the internet—from social media to online shopping to fantasy football, each with its own ways of shaping our everyday.

In the Grill Project (p.82), we explored the soft arrangement of how youth feel that if someone looks at you hard (grills you), you have to grill them back. It felt completely unchangeable to them. If they didn't grill back, they were a punk. We were trying to uncover and disturb the often dangerous daily arrangements and agreements about what it takes to "be a man" or prove your toughness (including for girls).

WHO DOES THIS DUDE THINK HE'S LOOKING AT?!?!

Since arrangements are both hard and soft, looking at and for social arrangements requires a fairly broad set of competencies. To make things more complex, arrangements are constantly intersecting and interacting. Think about two youth grilling each other. They are in the immediate arrangement of grilling, while simultaneously being in the hard arrangement of a school hallway, public bus, or street, in the soft arrangements of identity ("big brother," "butch dyke," "new kid"), or the multiple arrangements of hanging out with friends, heading to work, etc. In that sense, *effects are emergent properties of multiple overlapping hard and soft arrangements.* When we want to fight effects like "youth violence," we would do well to look at multiple arrangements: the overcrowded bus or school hallway, the lack of youth jobs or affordable transit, and even the agreements embedded in the grill.

Creating new effects—the ones we believe will make life more just and enjoyable—then calls for questioning, changing and re-imagining multiple arrangements. Just as activists call for intersectional thinking in how we think of ourselves and our struggles, we believe we need to understand the intersections of multiple hard and soft arrangements if we are going to truly challenge social injustices.

EFFECTS are emergent properties of multiple overlapping hard & soft arrangements.

EFFECTS

We use the term "effects" to talk about the impacts that ideas and arrangements have on our everyday life and larger world. These include the large scale effects of injustices based on racism, classism, sexism, etc.—effects like the achievement gap, vast income and health disparities, and the underrepresentation of women in the U.S. Congress. They also include the more mundane effects generated by everyday arrangements like public transit, men's and women's bathrooms, Facebook "likes," etc.

1) Effects are the big things we're always fighting against.

Effects are dramatic. They are everything from climate change related flooding to the police shootings of black people. They stir up our passions. They make us want to act. Effects are the things that make the news on one hand and are the topics of our conferences and meetings on another. Food scarcity, the opioid crisis, low literacy rates, school shootings (or closings), climate chaos, and gentrification all fall under the concept of effects in this framework.

On a brighter note, as we look to create change and address injustice, success can show up in a variety of big effects, some of which we can hardly imagine. These could range from soaring success rates for students in fully-resourced public schools, to zero police shootings in a city that disarms its police force, to an uptick in Gross National Happiness (GNH), the index put forward by the small nation of Bhutan to contrast with capitalism's obsession with the GDP (Gross Domestic Product).[1]

2) Effects are the little things we experience everyday.

We experience numerous effects all the time. We live them as good or bad outcomes of the arrangements of our world. They are the bus always running late, the stress of rent we can't afford, the water we can't drink, the lack of jobs for our kids, etc. They are the fight at school between kids who spent too long sitting in those rows, or the feeling of invisibility for folks of color in a city that whitewashes its public spaces and promotions. Conversely, they could be the good mood after playing basketball in a public park or the feeling of friendship after discussing your shared love of books with a fellow commuter.

With IAE, we inspect the small effects as much as we do the big ones. We hold them up to scrutiny, and speak to the meta-effects of the *accumulation* of small effects. What level of constant suspicion, surveillance and disrespect adds up to the "toxic stress" that contributes to the higher rate of heart conditions in the black community?[2] What combination of job discrimination, rent-going-through-the-roof and widespread homophobia leads to homelessness in the LGBT population? While we dedicate protests, nonprofits, campaign speeches and conferences to the meta-effects, how do we measure or make sense of the vastly different experiences we might have just getting to that protest or conference? *We posit that a deeper awareness of small effects will give us new ideas for interventions or even whole new arrangements.*

With I·A·E, we want to inspect the small effects as much as we do the big ones. We want to hold them up to scrutiny and speak to the meta-effects of the <u>accumulation</u> of small effects.

HOW
I-A-E
COMES
TOGETHER

(and wiggles around)

I-A-E is meant to be a useful framework for those of us looking for new ways to create change, be they new "levers" or points of opportunity, new approaches or even new arrangements. We find it helpful in catching us when we default to familiar arguments or put too much weight on a particular candidate or policy. Here are a couple ways that IAE helps us broaden our palette for understanding how to make and assess change.

Why I-A-E rather than I-P-E

Shaking the habit of thinking Ideas-People-Effects (I-P-E)

How We Arrange Ourselves and Each Other

Inspecting the ways we collude with power

When IAE is Multidirectional

Keeping an eye out for the nonlinear

Why I-A-E rather than I-P-E
Shaking the habit of thinking Ideas-People-Effects (I-P-E)

As humans, we are prone to thinking "I-**P**-E" or Ideas-PEOPLE-Effects. That means we tend to look for whom we can blame when we experience negative effects. This leads us to believe that effects emerge from the deficiencies of individuals, rather than flawed arrangements. Think about when you are waiting in line for a bus that's late, and everyone gets a little mad at everyone else. It is really easy to get irritated with the person who is talking too loud on the phone, or pushing, or who smells bad. But we tend *not* to ask the bigger questions about why there aren't more buses, why the roads are so crowded, or why more people can't walk to where they need to go.

It is this human propensity to think I-**P**-E that also leads us to blame individual people for their problems or ours: to blame parents for childhood obesity or individual cops for state-sanctioned violence. This leads us to "solutions" like healthy eating classes or police body cameras, rather than challenging the sturdy arrangements of our industrial food systems or criminal justice system. It also makes us think that individual people can solve their problems, or ours; as if someone who learned how to eat and cook correctly had any more of a chance of solving childhood obesity than President Obama did of solving the problems of a democracy founded on slavery and capitalism.

When we use I-**A**-E instead, it helps us inspect how ideas about health and safety (and race and gender) become embedded in a multitude of arrangements—from the fast food chains to the healthy eating class, from police forces to school-to-prison pipelines. It helps us both understand and question the intersections of those arrangements and how they define certain people as problems. It helps us stop hating the player and start hating the game. This is critical, because as arrangements age and join forces with other arrangements, they assume power as the given backdrops of our lives. Their survival becomes more important to themselves and others than the sets of people for whom they might not work. We can't let that discourage us. Using I-A-E can help us find new ways to challenge arrangements—and imagine new arrangements altogether—as methods that can lead to greater change.

How We Arrange Ourselves and Each Other
Inspecting the ways we collude with power

The ways we talk to each other, look at each other, think and feel about each other and ourselves is as much a product of ideas, arrangements and effects as chairs, buildings and other tangible arrangements of daily life. As we've said, arrangements are both hard and soft. For those of us concerned with social change, this means social life—and the myriad of soft arrangements within it—is a rich terrain for intervention.

We can use the IAE framework to inspect the presuppositions embedded in our speech and thought habits just as we use it to inspect how ideas are embedded in exterior arrangements of everyday life. How we think and talk, as well as who we talk to and who we listen to, are arrangements that produce effects: they arrange and limit who we are and who others can be in our world.

We arrange each other every time we enact categories of social hierarchy, which means pretty much every time we interact. We arrange ourselves in small, quotidian ways with assumptions embedded in a title (Mr.? Ms.? Mx?) or the sense that no title is needed at all, or with assumptions about interests, parenthood, education, or sexual orientation. Speech patterns follow, as varied as the man-to-man greeting of "Did you see the game last night?"

to the array of racial euphemisms from "at-risk" to "underserved" to "diverse," to the functions of who speaks and who listens in our earlier example of chairs in rows in a classroom. These kinds of speech acts go unexamined in our larger social lives, but they are not innocent. What kinds of essentialist claims get reified and projected outward? Whose priorities are reflected in the implicated social arrangements?

We arrange ourselves and each other in larger ways as well. When DS4SI came up with the idea of the Public Kitchen (p. 98), people assumed we meant a soup kitchen. They immediately perceived it as a service, and in so doing, they arranged the always-other, always-needy people who would use it. Even after we created a space that brought people together across culinary talents and economic backgrounds, our funders asked, "Did you do a participant evaluation?", not realizing that the very act of asking people to fill out that form would have meant arranging them into a category of service recipient or program participant.

Similarly, when organizing groups speak of "their base," they risk falling into thought habits that arrange the very people they are fighting for and with. If we think of our base only as a source of power that we need to "turn out" or "build up," or as a mass of victims of oppression, are we also able to see them as nuanced individuals who might have very different ideas about our work, their neighborhood, the issue at hand, or even what we serve to eat?

Another way we arrange entire communities is by making generalized assumptions about their expertise. Take the notion that people are "experts on their experience." This can begin as a useful approach to youthwork or community organizing: adults going to young people to truly ask them about their lived experiences, or organizers doing "one-on-ones" to listen to what the community cares about. This is important work even if we used to be youth ourselves, even if we are from that community, etc. But it is also the work of arranging people, unless we listen for a vast array of expertise. Do we expect youth to want to organize around "youth issues" like education, or can they be fired up about housing or interpretation services? Do we only expect community members to be experts on the challenges of life in their community, or can we also see them as experts in carpentry, systems-analysis, education or acting?

To address these ways that we arrange ourselves and others, we have to get better at seeing where our current speech, thought and communication habits collude with the world we are fighting against, collude with power. Sometimes it comes from overlapping arrangements—our arrangements of thought reinforced by positions of power: our role as supervisor, teacher, organizer or service provider. When our work puts us in charge of people, knowledge or resources, there are fixed choreographies that we slide into. We have to start with the realization that this is a familiar dance and ask ourselves, "What is this choreography of interaction doing to us and others? What does it afford and deny?" These dances might be fun (or at least convenient), but they impose presuppositions that we might not want to enact. If we are to imagine a new world, we must not only question the current one, but question how it has arranged our own habits of thought, speech and interaction with others.

How we think & talk, as well as who we talk to and who we listen to, are arrangements that produce effects.

When IAE is Multidirectional
Keeping an eye out for the nonlinear

I-A-E is a conceptual framework for understanding and engaging with each part of the equation—the ideas, the arrangements, the effects—as well as with the equation as a whole. It gives us a clearer sense of the entire terrain that we are intervening in, and with that, a wider set of options for creating change. That said, it is neither as clean nor as linear as it might appear. One thing we know about systems—both conceptual and literal ones—is that they can back up on you! So even as we keep in mind that "Ideas are embedded in Arrangements, which in turn yield Effects," we understand that the equation can go in all sorts of directions: Arrangements can yield new ideas. Effects can yield new arrangements, or even other effects, and so on. Here are a couple examples:

E-A-I: *Effects can generate new Arrangements which in turn lead to new Ideas*

Effects can provoke the addition of new arrangements to an already existing and unexamined set of arrangements. We can look back on our example of the arrangement of chairs as the primary learning tool in school. Sitting all day can lead some students to practically explode out of their young bodies—whether it's wiggling, giggling, jumping around, or even fighting. These students who can't sit in their

IDEAS

ARRANGEMENTS

EFFECTS

chairs and stay focused on the task at hand are frequently diagnosed as ADHD (Attention Deficit Hyperactivity Disorder) and prescribed medication like Ritalin or Adderall. Both the diagnosis and prescription were new medical arrangements added to the set of arrangements called chairs and school. We posit that there would be no diagnosis of ADHD if there was no social situation regulating and policing attention. However, the bodies which are out of compliance with the required means of demonstrating attention are more likely to bear the burden of the situation than the situation itself. "Fixing" out of line bodies with medication is easier than the work of changing the arrangements out of which the effects emerge.

Now the arrangements of ADHD and Ritalin give us new ideas about people. Now we have a new type of person, one unable to pay attention or stay still. This idea is so widespread that the term ADHD is frequently used in pop culture, including laypeople diagnosing themselves or others. Ian Hacking refers to this as "making up people" and uses examples of new categories of people from "obese" to "genius."

I have long been interested in classifications of people, in how they affect the people classified, and how the affects on the people in turn change the classifications. We think of many kinds of people as objects of scientific inquiry. Sometimes to control them, as prostitutes, sometimes to help them, as potential suicides. Sometimes to organise and help, but at the same time keep ourselves safe, as the poor or the homeless. Sometimes to change them for their own good and the good of the public, as the obese. Sometimes just to admire, to understand, to encourage and perhaps even to emulate, as (sometimes) geniuses. We think of these kinds of people as definite classes defined by definite properties. As we get to know more about these properties, we will be able to control, help, change, or emulate them better. But it's not quite like that. They are moving targets because our investigations interact with them, and change them. And since they are changed, they are not quite the same kind of people as before. The target has moved. I call this the 'looping effect'. Sometimes, our sciences create kinds of people that in a certain sense did not exist before. I call this 'making up people'. [3]

-Ian Hacking, *Making Up People*

A-I-E: Arrangements yield new Ideas that perpetuate Effects

Another example of arrangements giving us new ideas about people comes from the infernal arrangement of slavery. The arrangement of slavery came from ancient ideas of power and plunder in war, but the perpetuation of it in the "modern world" relied on generating new racist ideas about Africans. Indeed, well over a century after the abolition of slavery, racist ideas created by whites to justify slavery continue to be perpetuated. As Christina Sharpe wrote in her book *In The Wake: on Blackness and Being,* "Put another way, living in the wake [of slavery] means living in and with terror in that in much of what passes for public discourse *about* terror we, Black people, become the *carriers* of terror, terror's embodiment, and not the primary *objects* of terror's multiple enactments."[4] In other words, the racist ideas about black people in the U.S.—including the idea that they are dangerous—has had the effect of making them less safe and more likely to be the targets of violence, incarceration and even death.

So it is important to understand that I-A-E is not a formulaic route to action or linear order of events like cause and effect. It is a conceptual framework that can help us understand and act in new ways. To do so effectively requires us to keep our eyes out for its multiple variations and reconfigurations. It's tricky.

In closing, now that we've broken down what we mean by ideas, arrangements and effects, we want to reconnect them. As we said at the beginning:

Ideas are embedded in social arrangements.

> *"I'm often asked "Aren't tools neutral? Isn't it the intentions of users that matter?" As a semi-pro brick mason, I respond: I have seven different trowels. Each evolved for a specific task… I can't swap them out. If I forget my inch trowel and the building I'm working on has 1/4 inch joints, I'm screwed. How you use a tool isn't totally determined – you can use a hammer to paint a barn. But you'll do a terrible job. Tools are valenced, oriented towards certain ways of interacting with the world. Part of thinking well about technology and society is uncovering hidden valences and explaining how past development shapes a tool's present and future uses."* [5]

> –Political Scientist Virginia Eubanks

By using the I-A-E framework, we're asserting that ideas exist in the material world—in our trowels and classrooms and cars—as much as they exist in our cultural and personal worlds. Therefore, part of our work is to look at how ideas and beliefs are hidden in objects and situations, as well as the impact of the ecologies produced between these objects, situations and ourselves.

Arrangements produce effects.

"Imagine a man who is sitting in the shade of a bush near a stream. Suddenly he sees a child running by and realizes the child is in danger of falling into the stream. The man leaps from behind the bush and grabs the child. The child says, 'You ambushed me!' But the man replies, 'No, I saved you.'" [6]

— Social Psychologist Mindy Thompson Fullilove

The effects of the confusion between the man and the child seem to be produced by the actions of the man, but we would argue that there's also the bush! When the boy blames the man, it is akin to our example of the bus riders blaming each other for the smelly, noisy, overcrowded bus. Too often we focus on those who are "doing" or being "done to," rather than notice or question the concrete arrangements—bushes, busses, trowels—that are themselves doing. These hard arrangements overlap with soft arrangements (like expectations or schedules), and these overlapping arrangements produce effects.

For those of us fighting large-scale negative effects—those that grab the headlines or make our daily lives unbearable—it is counterintuitive to turn our eyes and actions away from them. We argue not so much for turning away from effects, but for the possibilities for change that arise when we dig into the arrangements that produce them.

How do we shift our focus to arrangements? And what new opportunities for creating social change open up when we do? Part Two will make the case that through honing our abilities to sense arrangements, intervene in them and imagine new ones, we will uncover new potential to build the world that we want.

part two
MAKING THE CASE FOR ARRANGEMENTS

Activists, artists, philanthropists, young people, academics—all manners of folks—constantly battle injustices and negative *effects* in their lives and others'. We take to the streets, to the internet, to the voting booth and more to fight for better outcomes. To the same degree, we argue vehemently about the *ideas* that underlie these injustices—from notions of public and private to ideas about categorizing our bodies, to all the isms that say some categories (and people) matter more than others.

But the arena for intervention that we at DS4SI want to make a case for is a less obvious one: that of the multiple, overlapping social arrangements that shape our lives. We believe that creating new effects—ones that make a society more just and enjoyable— calls for sensing, questioning, intervening in, and re-imagining our existing arrangements. ***Simply put, we see rearranging the social as a practical and powerful way to create social change.*** And we want those of us who care about social justice to see ourselves as potential designers of this world, rather than simply as participants in a world we didn't create or consent to. Instead of constantly reacting to the latest injustice, we want activists to have the tools and time to imagine and enact a new world.

As Michelle Alexander, author of *The New Jim Crow: Mass Incarceration in the Age of Colorblindness,* wrote in her 2018 debut op-ed for the New York Times:

Resistance is a reactive state of mind. While it can be necessary for survival and to prevent catastrophic harm, it can also tempt us to set our sights too low and to restrict our field of vision to the next election cycle, leading us to forget our ultimate purpose and place in history....Those of us who are committed to the radical evolution of American democracy are not merely resisting an unwanted reality. To the contrary, the struggle for human freedom and dignity extends back centuries and is likely to continue for generations to come.[7]

With the weight of lifetime Supreme Court appointments or health care or climate change seeming to hang in the balance of our elections, it is easy to get stuck there. But as Alexander points out, our fixation with politics and policies as the grand arrangement from which all other forms of social justice and injustice flow serves to "set our sights too low." When do we get to imagine the daily arrangements of "human freedom and dignity"?

We know this won't happen overnight. It takes time and investment for social arrangements to institutionalize and endure, and it will take time to change them. But it is critical that we try. And to do that, we need to be better at sensing arrangements, intervening in them and imagining new ones. This chapter will explore some examples of how DS4SI and others who inspire us have done this multi-tiered work:

exposing and poking at existing arrangements, as well as inviting people into collectively imagining new arrangements. In each case, we hope the examples function to both broaden the way activists see their work *and* to underscore for the larger public that arrangements are always re-arrangeable.

SENSING ARRANGEMENTS

1) *"Capitalism works for me!"*
2) *Space Bingo*
3) *Redlining the Adjacent Possible*
4) *"Is this chair one reason why...?"*

INTERVENING IN ARRANGEMENTS

1) *Mockus and the Mimes*
2) *The Grill Project*
3) *Lighting the Bridge*

IMAGINING NEW ARRANGEMENTS

1) *Wakanda: Imagining Africa Without Colonization*
2) *Social Emergency Response Center*
3) *Public Kitchen*

SENSING ARRANGEMENTS

It takes plenty of practice to develop a sense for identifying arrangements out in the world, or just under our noses for that matter. Sniffing out arrangements is akin to a boat captain sensing that there is a typhoon approaching, or a truffle hog honing in on fungus growing three feet below ground, or an exhausted traveler chasing a whiff of a fine batch of coffee brewing. They are all using their bodily sensory mechanisms trained to respond efficiently to environmental information. To build an analytical lens to start noticing and naming arrangements might take just as much training. We mean to hone multiple senses—not just sight!—as we stay alert for arrangements, much like the dreading boat captain, dutiful truffle hog and desperate weary traveler.

Sensing the social arrangements that shape our lives is the first step to deploying the I-A-E framework, but it can be harder than it sounds. They can be large or small, hard or soft, not to mention taken for granted, obscured, or overlapping. As we make a case for re-building our world through understanding Ideas-Arrangements-Effects, we believe sensing arrangements is the first step in breaking out of a world we take for granted.

Steve Lambert's "Capitalism Works for Me!" reminded passersby that their lives operated within the meta-arrangement of capitalism; it forced people to see an arrangement that often goes unquestioned.

Aware that capitalism deeply impacts our lives and yet is rarely spoken of directly, artist Steve Lambert created an intervention that both pointed to and questioned this meta-arrangement. Using the iconography of the flashy, lit up sign, Lambert invited folks to simply vote true or false to the sign's cheery statement: "Capitalism works for me!" In doing so, he created a spectacle that worked as both an attractor to engage the public and a simple invitation to weigh in—not on the merits of capitalism writ large, but on their own experience of it. As he described at the Creative Time Summit in 2012, the intervention "gives us room to imagine something else, [because it] transforms the thing that is largely unquestioned into a question." [8]

Space Bingo: Sensing the arrangements of physical space in our neighborhoods

Space Bingo participants went off in teams to different neighborhoods around Boston, with each team equipped with a Space Bingo board and Polaroid camera. They were challenged to capture the spaces they came upon that—to them—reflected the label of any given spot on the board.

We first designed Space Bingo for a cohort of youthworkers thinking about "out of school time" for young people. We wanted a tool that would help them think about "out of school space," and the impact the arrangements of space had on the young people traversing them. The game helped participants sense how terrains themselves were arranged and how they served to arrange the young people passing through them.

We have since played Space Bingo with all sorts of activists, and first and foremost it seems to help people literally see the arrangements of space around them. It is one thing to talk broadly about "gentrified neighborhoods" or "unsafe streets," but another to look at a new cafe and say "this is a space for a desired public" or look at a street clogged with cars, buses and bikes and say "this is a contested space." Ideas about people and neighborhoods and what people should and should not do in public are embedded in spatial arrangements, and these arrangements have effects. These spaces might make us believe we are the desirable or undesirable public, that we belong and should be protected or that we are as ugly as the prefab buildings and businesses that get zoned into poor neighborhoods.

This connects to:

1) Arrangements have effects. Arrangements of space can make us feel safe or unsafe, influence us to ride bikes or stay in our cars, invite us in or repel us (p.18).

2) Arrangements are both hard and soft. Participants in Space Bingo had to think about both the hard arrangements (streets, sidewalks, businesses, alleys) and the soft arrangements (looks, habits, fonts) that made them interpret these spaces as contested or welcoming or sanitized (p.32).

Redlining the Adjacent Possible:
Sensing the arrangements of the gig economy

	CONDEMNED	CONDONED
Apartment Share		
Bike Share		
Urban Chickens		
Micro-business		

In 2010 we were asked to write a paper about youth and the future of work. Our paper, *Redlining the Adjacent Possible: Youth and Communities of Color Face the (Not) New Future of (Not) Work*, focused on ideas around the "sharing economy." More specifically, we looked at how racist ideas—both big and small—inform which sharing arrangements are condemned and which are condoned.

The wild hyperbole and frenetic capitalizations of the new 'sharing' economy behemoths like Airbnb, Uber, WeWork, etc., obscure the fact that communities of color and poor communities have been in the sharing economy for centuries. With limited access to jobs, communities and young people of color have a long history of sharing, hustling, hacking, crowdfunding and most definitely redistributing. It just looks different, gets no funding, and is typically vilified as somehow illegal, illegitimate and/or immoral. Basically, if poor people and people of color are doing it, it is far more likely to be condemned than condoned, funded and celebrated.[9]

This connects to:

Ideas are embedded in social arrangements. By contrasting responses to similar social arrangements, we pointed out how racist ideas about people—both big, sturdy ideas and small, tricky ones—can get embedded in how their social arrangements are perceived, including whether they are declared illegal or invested in as the newest thing (p26).

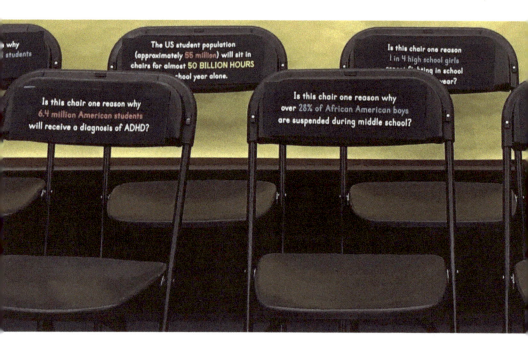

The US student population (approximately 55 million) will sit in chairs for almost 50 BILLION HOURS ...hool year alone.

Is this chair one reason 1 in 4 high school girls ... fighting in school ...ear?

Is this chair one reason why 6.4 million American students will receive a diagnosis of ADHD?

Is this chair one reason why over 28% of African American boys are suspended during middle school?

Students spend huge amounts of time in chairs, and yet they rarely come up in conversations about education justice. Why should chairs be our primary tool for learning? What are the impacts of having sitting be our predominant posture for learning? We wanted to question the role of the chair in a way that would help educators and students alike question a whole host of school arrangements.

We looked at chairs because they are such a prevalent and indicative arrangement of education. By putting statistics on chairs, we invited our audiences to hold these chairs accountable for things we usually blame teachers, parents, administrators and other students for. Focusing on the chairs, and assigning them culpability, was also a way into a different set of conversations about the ideas embedded in the chair as a learning tool. It enabled participants to explore assumptions about respect, paying attention, sitting straight, repetition and other pedagogical assumptions embedded in the arrangements of school. In short, it helped participants begin to talk about a whole host of underlying arrangements and assumptions that make up the school experience. And it created a small window into thinking about how schools might be re-arranged.

This connects to:

I-A-E not I-P-E. By helping start a conversation about questioning arrangements rather than blaming students, parents, and teachers, we created the chance for participants to think I-A-E (ideas-arrangements-effects) rather than I-P-E (ideas-people-effects) (p.46).

WHAT ARRANGEMENTS DO YOU SENSE IN YOUR EVERYDAY LIFE?

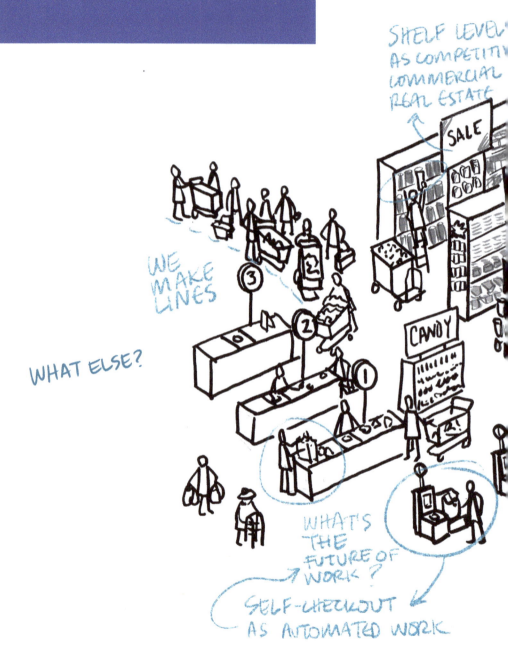

74

FROZEN FOOD FOR LONGEVITY & CONVENIENCE

ARRANGEMENTS OF FULL/PART TIME/ UNIONIZED WORK

PREPARED FOODS

FREE SAMPLES

ORGANIC

ARRANGEMENTS OF HEALTH, FARMING PRACTICES, SOCIAL STATUS

FRESH

ARRANGEMENT OF FOOD SOURCES NEAR & FAR

MARKETING TERMS/WORDS PLAYING ON OUR FOOD VALUES

TEMPTING SUGARY CEREAL AT KIDS' EYE LEVELS

INTERVENING IN EXISTING ARRANGEMENTS

Once we have a sense of the many overlapping arrangements at play in a situation, we can begin to shape interventions to instigate change. *When we talk about social intervention, we mean the act of interfering with a condition to modify it, or with a process to change its course.* Just as our boat captain, truffle hog and caffeine-deprived traveler were icons for sensing arrangements, we can take inspiration from the Ndembu doctor who intervened on an ill patient in such a way that it shifted the entire social dynamics of his village. First described by Victor Turner in *An Ndembu Doctor in Practice*, here it is summarized in anthropologist and cultural theorist Mary Douglas's book *Purity and Danger*:

The Problem

"The symptoms were palpitations, severe pain in the back and disabling weakness. The patient was also convinced that the other villagers were against him and withdrew completely from social life. Thus there was a mixture of physical and psychological disturbance."

The Interventionist

The Ndembu Doctor

The Intervention

"The doctor proceeded by finding out everything about the past history of the village, conducting séances with everyone in which everyone was encouraged to discuss their grudges against the patient, while he aired his grievances against them. Finally the blood cupping treatment dramatically involved the whole village in a crisis of expectation that burst in the excitement of the extraction of the tooth from the bleeding, fainting patient. Joyfully they congratulated him on his recovery and themselves on their part in it. They had reason for joy since the long treatment had uncovered the main sources of tension in the village. In future the patient could play an acceptable role in their affairs. Dissident elements had been recognised and shortly left the village for good. The social structure was analysed and rearranged so that friction was, for the time, reduced."

The Effects of the Intervention

"The back-biting and envy of the villagers, symbolized by the tooth in the sick man's body, was dissolved in a wave of enthusiasm and solidarity. As he was cured of his physical symptoms and they were all cured of social malaise. These symbols worked at the psycho-somatic level for the central figure, the sick man, and at the general psychological level for the villagers, in changing their attitudes, and at the sociological level in so far as the pattern of social statuses in the village was formally altered and in so far as some people moved in and others moved away as a result of the treatment." [10]

The Ndembu doctor's understanding of intervention meant that his intervention hit the individual (physical and psychological) register and the social/political one at the same time, so the tooth became the symbolic lever for a larger change. Successful social interventions don't often include pulling teeth, but they do point out unexpected points of convergence, and new levers for creating the kinds of change we seek.

When we talk about SOCIAL INTERVENTION, we mean the act of interfering with a condition to modify it, or with a process to change its course.

Mockus and the Mimes:
Intervening in the arrangements of civic culture

A philosophy professor and President of the National University of Colombia, Antanas Mockus was elected to be the Mayor of Bogota in the late 1990s and again in the early 2000s. He is perhaps best known outside of Colombia as the mayor who hired 420 mimes to replace his traffic cops. At that time Bogota was already a megacity, and its massive traffic woes wore on everyone—drivers, bus riders and pedestrians alike. Rather than making traffic more orderly and safe, traffic cops were notorious for issuing tickets just so they could take bribes from offending drivers.

After hearing from his traffic police and government advisors that there was nothing to do about Bogota's traffic chaos, Mayor Mockus fired his traffic cops and gave artists their jobs. With humor and teasing—rather than tickets and bribes—the system of street mimes as traffic facilitators intervened in the daily arrangements of traffic and bribes.

When Mockus talks about the impetus for this intervention in the city, he talks about his desire to build a sense of trust in the power of collective agreements. He wanted to give the people of Bogota an example of how following laws could actually benefit individuals and the city at large. His idea of traffic mimes invited another kind of citizen-to-citizen accountability, one that ultimately started to shift Bogota's larger civic culture.[11]

With humor and teasing—rather than tickets and bribes—the system of street mimes as traffic facilitators intervened in the daily civic arrangements of traffic and bribes.

The Grill Project:
Intervening in arrangements of violence

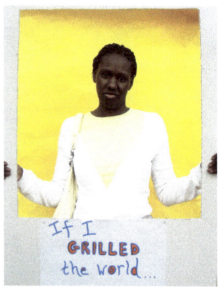

In the summer of 2009, we decided to take on "the grill"—
an arrangement in which two peers catch eyes and assume
animosity, often leading to threats or actual violence. As part
of our Youth Activism Design Institute (YADI), we interviewed
over 60 youth, and they all understood the grill and what it
required: if you got grilled by someone, you *had* to grill back.
If you didn't, you were considered a punk and risked constant
harassment. Each and every young person we spoke with thought
the power of the grill to demand reciprocation was something
that could never be dislodged; it was a moment in which they

felt that their whole reputation and future safety was on the line. This made us wonder: if we could mess with the *moment* of the grill, could we mess with the whole arrangement of grilling?

In partnership with 15 YADI interns that summer, we designed The Grill Project. In this intervention, the youth interns asked over 100 teens (and early 20-somethings) to give us their "best grill" as they posed holding a "life size Polaroid" frame (white foamboard, actually). This odd request made many youth falter to find their "best grill"—instead they laughed or smirked before pulling together their toughest look.

We felt we were beginning to surreptitiously challenge the arrangement of the grill, since the automaticity of its escalation depends on a certain kind of conceptual isolation. By playfully messing with the grill, we created a strange experience that might pop up and interrupt the next time the youth was grilled. Would they instantly grill back, or perhaps get distracted momentarily, thinking "damn, that's a good grill"? And for our interns, we might have introduced a glitch in the matrix of youth violence. If they saw that the grill was just an arrangement, what else might they question in the ways they were arranged, or arranged others? What other arrangements that resulted in violence might they intervene in? [12]

This connects to:

1) **We arrange ourselves and each other.** When we intervene in arrangements like the grill, we are inviting everyone to notice not only how we are arranged, but how we all collude in arranging ourselves and arranging each other (p.48).

2) The grill is an example of what we call **"the symbol and the thing"**—it is a real thing that we can poke at, as well as a symbol of the larger ecosystem of social violence (p.140).

Lighting the Bridge:
Intervening in an arrangement of placebreaking

Our 2014 intervention, "Lighting the Bridge" was an example of intervening in a hard arrangement, in this case a commuter rail bridge underpass on a busy street that was poorly lit and felt unsafe to passers-by. We intervened in this arrangement with a temporary, guerilla-style bridge lighting.

During our creative placemaking work in the Boston neighborhood of Upham's Corner, we recognized this underpass as a point of what we called "placebreaking." Without sufficient lighting, the bridge created a break between neighborhoods: it kept residents on one side from using the rec center on the other side, while residents on the other side didn't feel safe crossing to access the shopping district after dark. The darkness and associated danger of the bridge created a significant physical and visual divide for residents and deepened their belief that their neighborhood was "unsafe."

Over two evenings our installation of lights and an illuminated red carpet transformed the bridge into a bright, joyful space. People old and young walked, biked, and skipped on the red carpet. As people walked through, we gathered their comments on how lighting the bridge would transform their experiences and perceptions. It was clear that the need for more light was felt by everyone who came through and that this had been their sentiment for years. Following our unofficial temporary lighting, the city and a local foundation moved to hire a lighting artist to permanently light the way under the bridge. By intervening in an arrangement of placebreaking, we moved at least one step closer to an arrangement that transformed the bridge into a gateway rather than a barrier between neighborhoods.

This connects to:

1)Arrangements yield effects. The arrangement of a dimly lit bridge underpass had many effects— from pedestrians feeling unsafe to their lack of access to resources on the other side. By lighting the bridge—even temporarily—we allowed residents to feel the effects of connection and safety (p.18).

2) "Lighting the Bridge" was an example of what we call a **"productive fiction"**—an interactive chance to experience the world in a new way by creating a micro-space where that world already existed (p.143).

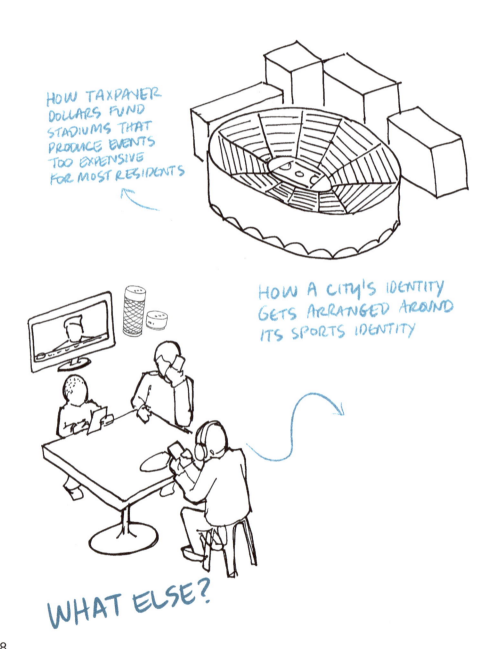

HOW TAXPAYER DOLLARS FUND STADIUMS THAT PRODUCE EVENTS TOO EXPENSIVE FOR MOST RESIDENTS

HOW A CITY'S IDENTITY GETS ARRANGED AROUND ITS SPORTS IDENTITY

WHAT ELSE?

HOW GOODS MOVE
ACROSS LAND AND
SEA AT THE CLICK
OF A MOUSE

IMAGINING NEW ARRANGEMENTS

Entangled with the acts of sensing and intervening in existing arrangements is the challenge to articulate different arrangements. These new visions are not necessarily prescriptive; they aren't "we-should-do-this-instead-of-that." Rather they are meant to be a starting point, something that others can play off of, collaborate with or improve on. Far from the boat captain or truffle hog whose sensing skills come from familiarity and repetition, our icons here are more the early hip-hop DJs who created a new music genre (and dance scene) by manipulating the records themselves, or the chefs riffing off of various culinary heritages to create new fusion food styles. Like DJing and cooking, imagining new arrangements is always a participatory exercise, one which relies on inspiration and creativity, but also the keen ability to sense the flow of ideas, moves, sounds and tastes as a way of collaborating with all kinds of people.

Cosplay of Black Panther, Storm and the forces of Wakanda, at Dragon Con 2013 in Atlanta, GA.

Brought gloriously to life in the blockbuster Marvel movie *Black Panther*, Wakanda is an imagined African nation that was never colonized. With its own resources and intelligence, Wakanda and its citizens became the most technologically advanced country in the world. Wakanda presents a counter image that helps us see the current effects of the arrangement of colonialism. That is, seeing Wakanda as a possibility begs the question "What would Africa—and the world—be like without colonialism?"

Authors Stan Lee and Jack Kirby's imaginings of this place—along with the spectacular renderings in both the comic book and movie—created a beautiful jumping off point for this question. Millions of moviegoers got to see some of the most exciting possibilities for imagining new takes on both Africa and the Black Diaspora. When the movie's enormous success blew Hollywood away, it just added to the euphoria and sense of possibility. New arrangements for cities, power sources, languages and even types of people came instantly into view.

Social Emergency Response Centers (SERCs): Imagining a new community-led arrangement to respond to social emergencies

In emergencies like hurricanes, fires and floods, emergency response centers are a state-sponsored arrangement created to provide temporary services like housing, food, water and information. In the fall of 2016, we invited others to join us in re-imagining this arrangement to take on the real and pressing *social emergency* that we were facing—frrom state-sanctioned violence against Black communities, to gentrification, Islamophobia, privatization, environmental devastation, and more. Our first SERC opened in Boston the weekend after Trump's inauguration. It was packed with close to 300 neighbors, artists, activists, health professionals, families, academics, city workers and spiritual leaders.

SERCs are an imagined arrangement, a DIY public infrastructure that any community can use when they need it. They are co-created with activists, artists and community members alike. Far from the sterile arrangements of an emergency response center, a SERC might smell like fresh ink on paper from printmaking or the sweat of a dance class, taste like fried yucca or moqueca, and sound like taiko drumming or a story circle.

To support this fledgling arrangement, we created a SERC Manual and SERC Kit to share with communities that wanted to launch their own SERCs. Indeed, dozens of SERCs have been launched both nationally and internationally, in spaces and communities as diverse as a bookstore in London, Ontario, a policy conference in Chicago, a Mutual Aid Liberation Center in South Atlanta, and a home in tiny Dardelle County, Arkansas.

This connects to:

1) It's nonlinear: A-I (A new arrangement that creates new ideas). One of the key elements of the SERC as a new arrangement is how it helps people understand the idea of the social emergency. By using the frame of the social emergency and the metaphor of an emergency response center, the SERC places urgency on our understanding that seemingly disparate events are in fact deeply bound together. It also creates space for participants to begin reconstruction: imagining how to build a stronger, more just democracy (p.52).

2) Amplifying the Unspoken. By creating a Social Emergency Response Center, we were amplifying the unspoken—and often unrealized—reality that we are in a social emergency. Our aim was to move beyond reacting to each new atrocity as if it were a one-off and to move into understanding the connections between racism, police violence, displacement, vote stealing, immigrant bashing, and more (p.138).

Public Kitchen:
Re-imagining the public through imagining a new public infrastructure

Public Kitchen is a "productive fiction" that invites community residents to experience a not-yet-existing public infrastructure—or arrangement, if you would—that could make their daily lives more vibrant, affordable, tasty and healthy. Inspired by the family kitchen as a gathering place, the first Public Kitchen was an indoor-outdoor installation in the Boston neighborhood of Upham's Corner, where over 600 residents joined us in a week of fresh food, cooking competitions, a mobile kitchen, recipe sharing, food-inspired art, food justice conversations, and much more.

The Public Kitchen—which has since popped up from Vancouver, Canada to Tasmania, Australia—is an imagination project aimed at addressing the stigma of things that are "public," while also capturing the imaginary about how a strong public infrastructure can change our lives. Public Kitchen poses the question "If kitchens were public—like libraries, schools and basketball courts—how could it rearrange social life?"

Public Kitchen was neither a soup kitchen nor a charity (although it fed hundreds of people for free); it was an entirely new arrangement. It moved away from the *ideas* of poverty and wretchedness that get embedded in the arrangement of soup kitchens, moving towards ideas of sharing, conviviality and the public as a work in progress. It was a prototype of a new infrastructure, a way to say that when we explore new forms of sociality, we can create new ways of seeing and arranging each other and possibly even become new categories of subjects.

© Travis Watson Photography

This connects to:

1) We arrange ourselves and each other.
When we invited folks to join us at Public Kitchen, they frequently slid into assuming that the people who should come were poor people who needed food. The reality of the intervention created space for new arrangements between people who may or may not have been poor, but who were also neighbors, food justice advocates, amateur chefs, gardeners, etc. (p.48).

2) Productive fiction.
Public Kitchen is a classic example of a productive fiction—a DS4SI intervention technique aimed at engaging the public in imagining the future we want, by creating a small glimpse of it as if it already exists (p.143).

WHAT NEW ARRANGEMENTS CAN YOU IMAGINE IN THIS SCENE?

COME TO OUR BLOCK PARTY!! JUNE 10

WHAT ELSE?

CAFE
4-10PM

"ROTATING CAFE" WHERE ASPIRING LOCAL ENTREPRENEURS COULD TEST THEIR IDEAS

WHAT IF THIS ROOF HAD A GIANT MATTRESS?

STAR GAZE CLUB

ARRANGEMENTS WHERE WE CAN VOTE ON THINGS BESIDES CANDIDATES, LIKE THE BUDGET, OR WARS OR POLICIES

"DANCE COURT" AS AN ARRANGEMENT SO IT'S AS EASY TO PUT ON A DANCE PARTY IN PUBLIC AS IT IS TO PLAY BALL

RAISED PROTECTED BIKE LANES

In short, we see arrangements as the sweet spot between ideas and effects. They are a powerful and often overlooked way that ideas take up agency and act upon us. In other words, **arrangements help ideas arrange us.** And we argue that all kinds of arrangements— social, political, spatial, etc.—are the primary culprits in the production of the negative effects that we are so often fighting against, as well as the lack of positive effects that we are yearning for. Not only can changing arrangements improve bad effects, they can produce unimagined good ones. In other words changing arrangements can change us.

How do we change arrangements? What tools can we use to redesign the social? Part Three will make a case for having an impact at the scale of the social, as well as sharing some of the design tools we've created for this work.

part three

DESIGNING THE SOCIAL

"Another world is possible."
World Social Forum slogan

"Changing how social justice is imagined, developed and deployed in the U.S."
Excerpt from Mission Statement, DS4SI

"The everyday is always a question, a problem." [13]
Ben Highmore, *Everyday Life and Cultural Theory*

We use the term "the social" to mean the contested and always changing terrain of social life. To us the social is neither static nor innocent. We use "sociality" to point to how the social is constantly being produced and enacted: created through numerous practices that have to do with meaning (and often with power), such that our collective experiences are both historically based and always changing. In I-A-E design terms, we would say that through our arrangements, we both co-construct "the social" and are constructed by it. This section makes the case for the power of redesigning the social, as well as sharing specific ways to use social interventions to dive into this work.

A CASE FOR THE SOCIAL

A CASE FOR DESIGN

DESIGNING THE SOCIAL

A CASE FOR SOCIAL INTERVENTION

DESIGNING SOCIAL INTERVENTIONS

Design Research

Social Intervention Design

Prototyping

Evaluation

A CASE FOR THE SOCIAL

Dear Friends,

We thought now would be a good time to check in with you. We want to make the leap from exploring our framework of I-A-E to putting it into action yourselves. We think it's useful then to check back in with our challenge to you to think as world builders. To us this means we need to take on the larger domain of social life, the domain we've ceded all too much to Silicon Valley and Hollywood. This kind of expanding our presence and command within the social need not require that we mimic the kinds of growth strategies currently employed by those corporate entities. We're not looking for a franchise model of expansion or a sterile model of contact. We can imagine a kind of reach that cultivates and celebrates site specific differences, that reclaims sociality such that joy is not equal to purchasing power and articulation of self is not considered branding. We're talking about a kind of wilding of sociality where forms of identification and conviviality aren't the total domain of the corporate sector.

Here are a couple places you might start:

1)   Start by looking IN:

One place to practice this kind of audacity might take place "within" our work to start. If we are to play a larger role and take a stronger presence in the making of everyday life, we'd need to tackle rearranging our work and our goals. Currently our ideas about social justice and injustice have been departmentalized, shaping the arrangements of siloes within our work that further reduce and compartmentalize our impact. We speak of intersectionality in our identities and struggles, and then head off to separate conferences or protests or art pieces about race, class, gender or sexuality. Where is the room for our complex, social selves? There's very little collective space for simply making sense of the larger social and cultural world that we are trying to alter and affect.

But we are not just suggesting a conference which has more room for complexity or invites more types of participants. Conferences themselves are a limiting arrangement—with their own sub-arrangements of speakers and listeners (with its inherent emphasis on verbal communication), fees, locations, funders, etc. We need to question each of the arrangements of our work, from our personal interactions, to the content, forms, and tempos of our convenings, to our notions of success or even evaluation. How can we rearrange ourselves to be more outward facing, which will require a new series of interactions with our larger publics?

2)   Start by looking OUT:

We think an interesting place to start is looking out into public life and thinking about phenomena that touch everyone, directly or indirectly—that give shape to social life, but also that interest you as a person. What's that conundrum you'd like permission to address? Is it that social life in your city shuts down after 10 pm? Or that the only place to buy food in your rural area is at dollar stores? Is it all the tax payer dollars that went into that shiny new stadium? Or that all the local radio stations are in English? We believe we could think way more broadly in terms of how we address these phenomena. We want us all to think of this as within our bailywick and to not limit our role to protesting or meeting or creating art work about a given thing. Let's look at the people we call our constituency, and all the people they work, live and play with. We often think of them either when we want to turn them out to something or we are worried about them (based on new legislation, politicians, etc.). But what about when they're having a great time? What about wondering what we can learn from them? If we shift our arrangement with our base, what could that bring to nightlife, or public space, food culture or radio? How long would it take until we were the ones programming at the scale of the stadium?

Wherever you want to start, we encourage you to think across scale and direction. Remember when Cuba decided that it needed a doctor and nurse responsible for every neighborhood? Or when labor unions brought us the weekend? What profound re-arrangement can you imagine? We hope **Part One and Two** help make this kind of re-arranging seem doable, and we hope **Part Three** helps you step into your power as a designer of everyday life.

cheers,
DS4SI

A CASE FOR DESIGN

Everyone designs who devises courses of action aimed at changing existing situations into preferred ones.[14]

- Herbert Simon, *The Sciences of the Artificial*

In a world in rapid and profound transformation, we are all designers…. [T]he "all" we are talking about includes every subject, whether individual or collective, who in a world in transformation must determine their own identity and their own life project. This means putting their design capability into action: a way of thinking and doing things that entails reflection and strategic sense, that calls us to look at ourselves and our context and decide whether and how to act to improve the state of things.[15]

- Ezio Manzini, *Design, When Everybody Designs: An Introduction to Social Innovation*

Why did DS4SI choose design as our approach to creating change at the scale of the social? The practice of design—whether one is designing tools or buildings, sneakers or social interventions—is deployed to fix existing problems and/or to manifest what does not yet exist. As such, design is both problem solving and world building. It helps propel us beyond merely addressing existing problems with existing forms (sound familiar?) into imagining entirely new terrains of possibility.

DS4SI believes that design includes a set of tools and skills that we as activists should use as readily as our planning, facilitation and evaluation tools. Within our current fields of practice, we share a fairly mutual understanding of planning and its importance, whether it's strategic planning, project planning, class planning, etc. In the same vein, we share a broad understanding of evaluation as a set of tools meant to help us answer the question, "Is what we're doing working?" However we don't have the same kind of shared understanding and collective value placed on design, which for us happens before we have something to plan and evaluate. To us, design is what we do to help determine the course of action.

Design invites widely disparate ways of knowing into a single co-creative practice. It is about bringing together divergent ways of making sense of a situation or a problem: inviting ways of thinking that might feel contradictory to, or far afield from, our own ways of seeing an issue. It should jostle our own assumptions about a problem. When it's done in product design, it might help a footwear company come up with an amazing new basketball sneaker by pulling in insights from players ("users"), but also from car makers, graphic illustrators and toy designers. Ideas about new priorities, materials or styles could surface from this interesting collection of perspectives. When we're thinking about problem solving, this is akin to Antanas Mockus going to his government leaders and traffic experts but also to his artist community to come up with his radical "traffic mime" approach to taking on Bogota's massive traffic problem (p. 80).

The designer's stance is experimental and curious, which can feel like a luxury to activists or advocates who frequently feel like we have to say we totally understand a problem and know the solution (which we will carry out if we have a) power or b) funding). This is what drew us to design and made us open the Studio. We were weary from years of familiar solutions—marches, programs, policies, meetings. Our experiences trying to come up with new ideas with community residents and youth made us realize that imagining new solutions is more than just being asked. It requires a set of tools that helps people think more divergently. We found some of those tools in the design world, and the rest we created ourselves, including the Intervention Design Tools coming up later in this section (p. 137).

At the Studio we bring together different kinds of thinkers—what we might call "art thinkers," "social thinkers" and "change thinkers." (Understanding of course, that many of us think across types.) For us art thinking brings knowledge of symbol, passion and aesthetics into the fray for how we make sense of a problem. Social thinking brings knowledge of social sciences, social theory and philosophy, and with it an understanding of how belonging, mattering, history and ecologies add to people's sensemaking of a problem. Change thinking includes the knowledge of how power works, how to challenge it and build the collective belief, leadership and bravery to do it. It adds an understanding of the relationship between power and identity, the complexity of intersectionality and how power and oppression play out across our multiple identities. Again, we don't put these types of knowledge out there as monolithic, since many people identify as both artists and social theorists or activists and academics. However, understanding these different kinds of knowledge helps us ensure variety in thinking as a practice for finding new ways into problems.

One example of this was how partnering with Judith Leemann (fiber artist and professor at Massachusetts College of Art and Design) opened up new lines of thinking about social violence for us and a group of young people during the summer of the Grill Project (p. 82). All of the youth had experienced and witnessed violence. Many felt they deeply understood it, and many had been a part of traditional approaches to decreasing it, from youth programs and summer jobs to school discipline and police run-ins. Judith led sessions on analogical thinking as a way to get young people in a frame from which to imagine. When she invited youth to map out violence as if it were a basketball game, they ended up wondering about the adult "coaches" and "refs" who facilitate youth violence. When they mapped out violence as going out to eat with friends, they questioned the "doggy bag" you take leftovers home with—"It's your reputation!" shouted one youth. Judith's "art thinking"—her understanding of metaphor and aesthetic—opened us up in how we articulated both the dynamics at play within the grill and the dynamics at play in effective interventions. It created the opportunity for us to design a social intervention that addressed violence in a way that none of us had seen before.

We believe that design's strength is in its invitation to broaden and complicate our thinking. Our willingness to stay open and curious, along with some good design practices, can help us uncover new solutions to the problems we are facing, even for folks who have spent their lives experiencing them and taking them on. When we revisit our original case for this book, that "ideas are embedded in social arrangements that in turn produce effects," we believe that design tools can help us dig through these layers, even within the hectic, joyful, messy terrain of everyday life.

DESIGNING THE SOCIAL

When moved to create change, people tend to begin by addressing problems at the level of (negative) effects: urgently fighting gentrification, unclean water, police violence, lack of access to good schools and jobs, etc. At DS4SI, we use design research tools to *reset the problem* at the scale of social arrangements, in order to create a problem frame that involves a larger scale of people and invites change in ways that could be broader, deeper or more transformative.

Of course the description and political framing of a social problem inevitably creates its own effects. As we say, "description embeds prescription"[16] (from Douglas Flemons' book *Completing Distinctions*). We have to be extremely careful when we frame or describe a problem, since in many ways it involves taking ideas about the people and the spaces evidencing the problem and using them to arrange the actual problem. And that arrangement—or description—bring with it prescriptions for how we interact with the problem and attempt to solve it. If your description is about people (I-P-E) rather than the arrangements that the problem flows from (I-A-E), you may be headed in the wrong direction (p. 46). We've seen this from the devastating effects of such problem frames as "superpredators," "crack babies" and "blighted neighborhoods," with the devastation always happening to the people and places that have been described as the problem itself.

After using design research to reset the problem at the scale of arrangements, we *design interventions* that point to deeper solutions through changing arrangements or ideas. One example of how we did this was when we worked with the Praxis Project to reframe the problem of "childhood obesity." This description had captured the medical institutional imaginary such that it was willing to criminalize children's bodies, blame and punish parents, all while turning a blind eye to the arrangements and larger systemic causes of obesity. The Praxis Project received funding to address childhood obesity in communities of color but explicitly used the approach of having community-led organizing groups fight for food justice and recreation equity. We used our Public Kitchen intervention (p. 98) to model how food justice—and community vibrancy—could be improved by framing the problem as an arrangement problem and engaging community members in imagining how a new public arrangement could change social life. From finding the point of intervention to coming up with and carrying out these interventions, we are always looking to challenge arrangements in ways that transform people's ideas about themselves and sociality. One interesting "start by looking in" version of this was when a number of thought-partners took on the social justice sector's various arrangements of silo-ed meetings and strategy sessions. Led by Project South (a Southern-based leadership development organization), they sought to create a more open and community-responsive arrangement that would embody the idea that everyone has important knowledge to share about identifying problems and creating solutions. Inspired by the social movement assemblies of the global South, they designed the "Peoples Movement Assembly." It has grown to be a nimble and frequently used form that invites people in across organizations, networks and frontlines to collectively engage in a process of identifying problems, surfacing solutions and committing to action. The "PMA" is an intervention that has been able to break through some of the entrenched hierarchies of organizing work, transforming people's ideas about their role in collective solution generation and accountability.

We know that the notion of "designing the social"

(inspired, in part by Bruno Latour's book *Reassembling the Social*), is beyond the scale of DS4SI, or any individual, artist crew, or underfunded nonprofit, for that matter. Nevertheless, we believe it's essential for people who care about social justice to see themselves as designers of everyday life. Since the scale and distribution of entrenched ideas and arrangements make it impossible for us to manipulate them by ourselves, (the way we can manipulate objects in our living room, say), we use social interventions as signals, suggestions and invitations to galvanize others into this work of rearranging and changing ideas and relations.

A CASE FOR SOCIAL INTERVENTION

Social interventions are a critical tool for designing the social, because they can shine a light on and interrupt current arrangements in ways that radically help us see what needs to be rearranged. Even as activists try to trace effects back to root causes, we frequently miss the daily social arrangements that do so much to reproduce the problem. *Intervening at the scale of arrangements helps us get to solutions that might be more robust or transformative, while also reminding us that re-arranging the social is both possible and required.*

When you move from addressing effects to challenging arrangements, you make an exponential move. Everything expands along multiple dimensions. For example, you expand from addressing "police violence against the black community" as a problem for blacks—and a problem of certain police— to addressing it as a civil society problem that we are all implicated in. What combination of ideas and arrangements of masculinity, security, white fragility, the law and "the other" make police violence an emergent property? It's like a jump in consciousness from the square to the cube.

When we move from the square to the cube, we have a much more complex job in front of us. We have to map and address

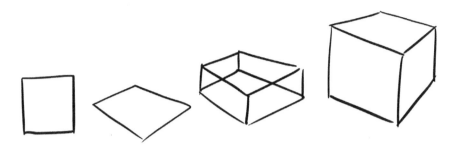

the set of hard and soft arrangements out of which state-sanctioned violence against communities of color emerges. We have to do the type of terrain research that broadens the question—that opens the lens up enough to help us find a more powerful point of leverage. Ideally the point of intervention will be a point where people and things that appear innocent are as implicated in the effect as the specific police and victims are. We want to find points of intervention that cross multiple thresholds or are at the interstices between arrangements.

With the intervention "Don't Shoot in Our Name," DS4SI experimented with a gesture of solidarity that would challenge the unspoken beliefs about who the police are meant to protect and serve. It invited people who were not directly on the frontlines of police violence to take a stand, to say that the wanton killing of black people was not something they would tolerate in the name of their own privileged safety. In so doing, it aimed at addressing police violence as a larger dimension than any particular police shooting; it was aimed at the unspoken cultural agreement of state sanctioned violence. An intervention at the scale of that agreement functions to invite the larger public into questioning other arrangements that lead to police and vigilante violence, arrangements like gun laws, police hiring and firing practices, our larger judicial system, etc. It also creates a window into questioning the *ideas* embedded in state-sanctioned violence, such as ideas about white dominance, social control and punishment. As you can see, the cube gets quite challenging, but also quite powerful.

In 2014, DS4SI invited passersby to pose with "Don't Shoot in My Name" written on their outstretched hands. It was a gesture done in solidarity with the frontline "Hands Up, Don't Shoot!" gesture in Ferguson, MO.

DESIGNING SOCIAL INTERVENTIONS

Sometimes a truly effective social intervention can feel like a trick itself—think of that moment when it opens our mind to an existing arrangement that we've always taken for granted or a new one we've never imagined, whether it's the humor of traffic mimes or the good vibes of collective cooking in a Public Kitchen. Effective social interventions invite us into new possibilities for who we can be and how we can shape the world around us.

That said, social interventions are as prone to our own mistakes as any other means of creating change. This section shares what we have learned along the way as we've studied, written about and tried our fair share of social interventions. We break the process down into three parts: design research, social intervention design and evaluation.

Action Lab, New Orleans

Action Lab, Detroit

We created Action Labs to help people design social interventions

Design Research

Design research includes digging into the context of the problem in order to unearth multiple understandings of it and to look for the arrangements that are producing it. In addition, design research can help locate a key element or lever for intervention.

Design Research Techniques:
- Terrain Research
- User Research
- Conceptual Research
- Participatory Action Research

AIDS Quilt Example:

In 1985, hundreds of gay men were dying from AIDS in San Francisco. Local activist Cleve Jones and his friends hung a "patchwork" of posters with the names of AIDS victims on the San Francisco Federal Building after a candlelight march. This patchwork reminded Cleve of a quilt (p. 142).

Social Intervention Design Evaluation

Social intervention design shapes how we will amplify our key element to intervene in an arrangement or invite others to co-imagine a new one.

Intervention Design Techniques:
- Amplifying the Unspoken
- The Symbol & the Thing
- Productive Fictions

Prototyping Social Interventions

When we evaluate our intervention across I-A-E (and not just effects), we get a broader sense of what did and didn't work. This leads us back to more design research to improve our intervention.

Evaluation Questions
- I-A-E Questions
- Design Research Questions

Cleve Jones and fellow activists invited people to make 3'x6' panels that commemorated loved ones who had died from AIDS. The prototype was the original quilt squares that Cleve and others made. The tremendous response of squares flooding in from all over the U.S. (and then the world) showed that the prototype spoke to people.

The profound ways that the AIDS Quilt changed ideas about people with AIDS went on to impact policies and other significant arrangements (health care and anti-discrimination policies, for example).

Design Research

When people are moved to take on complex social problems, they are usually moved by the profound negative *effects* these problems are producing: effects such as police shootings, homelessness, the immigration crisis, the opioid epidemic, the achievement gap, etc. For obvious reasons, negative effects such as these often shape the work and urgency of activists and communities most impacted by complex problems.

Even for folks who have experienced the effects first hand, **design research** can help unveil a more nuanced sense of the problem or help us see it in a new way. It can also lead to a deeper understanding of the arrangements that create the effects we are addressing. Finally, it is usually during our design research phase that we find a "key element" or symbol that we can amplify with our social intervention. Think of Steve Lambert's "Capitalism Works for Me!" (p. 66), and how he realized that a flashy, lit up sign could symbolize so much about capitalism, marketing and consumerism.

Designers usually call the time we spend looking at the problem and its context the "discovery phase." We always begin with discovery, but it is also important to revisit it multiple times in our design process. Some design research tools we use during this phase include: User Research, Terrain Research, Conceptual Research and Participatory Action Research.

Design Research

USER RESEARCH
Grill Project

TERRAIN RESEARCH
The 50' Bench

CONCEPTUAL RESEARCH
IAE Tool

PARTICIPATORY ACTION RESEARCH
Let's Flip It

User Research

We believe user research is a critical part of our initial design thinking when we are setting or solving a problem. We use qualitative methods like user interviews, user observations and interactive user experiences. This gives us a deeper understanding of how people are experiencing the problem we are trying to address—or if we are even addressing the correct problem! It doesn't stop there, however, as user research is frequently a part of the process all the way through our intervention design.

Example—The Grill Project
When we began our summer Youth Activism Design Institute, youth wanted to take on the violence between youth that was killing some of their loved ones. They set the problem as "youth violence." Our interviews with youth and youthworkers in the neighborhoods where we were going to be working led us to the role of "the grill" in starting violence between youth. It was fascinating to us that almost all the youth we interviewed said that if you were grilled, you had to grill back. That led us to choose it as a new point of intervention (p.82).

Terrain Research

By "terrain" we mean both the literal, physical terrain that we are thinking about intervening in as well as the social/political terrain. When we do physical terrain research in a neighborhood, we begin with observations at different times of day and night: we note sounds, sights and patterns of the space and its users. We walk the space, drive and take public transportation. We talk with the neighborhood's residents, merchants, and passersby about how and when they use the space, making sure to include youth and elders, new immigrants in the neighborhood, etc. When we think about a space's social and political life, we look at who is in the center of the space and who is in the margins, who is seen as desired users versus undesired ones, who attends meetings about the space, who sets formal and informal rules about the space, etc.

Example—The 50' Bench
When we were asked to do creative placemaking around the commuter rail stop in Boston's Four Corners neighborhood, the local community development corporations (CDCs) that hired us earnestly wanted more residents to use the stop. However, as we observed the (underused) station area and busy neighborhood nearby, we spotted many commuters sitting on a long pipe waiting

for the bus. While doing placemaking activities that highlighted the commuter rail, we also built a temporary bench over a short part of the pipe. It immediately and consistently got used. This led a local Artist in Residence, Claudia Paraschiv, to work with Maddu Huacuja and other neighborhood artists, residents and merchants to build a beautiful fifty foot long bench along the whole pipe. Her twelve week process of co-designing and building the bench incorporated ongoing research as well, an example of how often these techniques flow together.

DS4SI's initial 6' bench inspired local artists, residents and merchants to create "Seats of Power + Codex IV Corners," a 50' bench complete with games, plants and even music. (Led by Artist in Residence Claudia Paraschiv)

Conceptual Research

People's ideas about a problem can have as much influence on its sturdiness as any other cause we might conjecture. Conceptions can include assumptions about causes of a problem, beliefs about the people facing the effect, obliviousness to the arrangements at play, etc. Conceptual research helps us dig into this more hidden terrain.

Example—I-A-E Tool
When the Cambridge Education Association (a local teachers union in Cambridge, MA) invited us to engage their teacher-organizers in taking on pernicious racism in a system outwardly committed to ending racism, we jumped at the chance. What conceptions of Cambridge's students (and parents) contributed to racial inequities? What arrangements were at play formally and informally that embodied Cambridge's ideas about excellence or achievement? We designed this "I-A-E Tool" to help their organizers move from the inequities they were facing to some of the deeper ideas and arrangements that they were entrenched in. In small groups they chose an effect they were taking on ("unequal suspension and expulsion rates") and walked it back through arrangements at play (police in schools, chairs as primary learning tools, etc.) and then on to some of the ideas embedded in those arrangements (ideas about safety, obedience, boys of color, etc.)

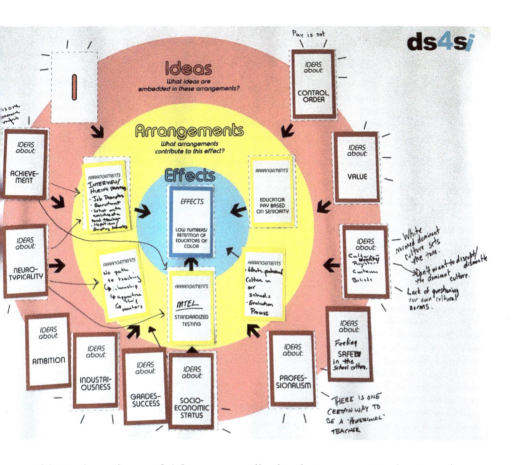

This tool can be useful for anyone digging into conceptual research of the effects they've surfaced, including exposing the diversity of arrangements at play and how they obscure some of the ideas that are embedded in them. Similar to how effective social interventions broaden our understanding of who is implicated by a social problem, this tool can help broaden the terrain from familiar conversations about school "adjustment officers" to hidden ideas of about order, civility or neurotypicality.

Any situation involving human beings is more than likely a hot mess with multiple moving targets.

"To study a situation one has to enter it and try and keep a clear head, for critical situations are usually confusing to all concerned. One then finds one is involved in a process, because the situation changes as soon as one has entered it." [17]

- From *Laing and Psychotherapy* by John M. Heaton

Psychiatrist RD Laing was concerned with the study of people in situations, especially people in social crises. Crucial to this was his insight that no one in the situation knows what the situation is; the situation has to be discovered. The stories people tell about the situation do not tell us simply and unambiguously what the situation is—there is no reason to believe or disbelieve a story because someone tells it. As we plan multilayered interventions (with multilayered real people), complexity pushes us to the edge of our craft.

Know the order in which you intend to intervene.

"As a game designer you can never directly design play. You can only design the rules that give rise to it. Game designers create experience but only indirectly." [18]

- From *Rules of Play,* by Katie Salen and Eric Zimmerman

There are first order interventions (addressing things you can get at directly) and second order interventions (addressing things you can't get at directly). Thinking about Salen and Zimmerman's description of game design as second order intervention can be helpful as we think about our own interventions. So, "we need more people" could lead to "let's do more recruitment" (first order), while "we need people to think more urgently about climate change" definitely requires second order intervention. It will require changing our relationships to concepts, beliefs, each other, and our environment. In fact it could require a change in us as much as in them. This move to deep relational change is second order.

Participatory Action Research

Participatory action research is a process that aims to engage people in investigating their own reality in order to change it.[19] We often use elements of participatory action research (PAR) in our user, terrain and conceptual research. For us, engaging a wide array of community members in exploring and defining the problem is a rich and useful part of our process. There is a widespread notion that people are experts on our lived reality. In fact, we're not! Indeed, engaging a community that is deeply impacted by a problem in a serious inquiry about that problem can lead to new ideas about solutions, or a new awareness about the arrangements that the problem flows from.

Example—Let's Flip It
Building on the work of the Grill Project (p. 82), our next summer's Youth Activism Design Institute participants decided to take on another element of youth culture that they felt led to youth violence. They identified how logos on sports caps were being used to communicate membership in turf based gangs, crews and cliques. They interviewed over 75 youth on the street or in youth-led

focus groups, and ended up deciding that a blank, all white, fitted cap could represent a decision to step away from block versus block violence, without its wearer having to step away from his (or her) block. "Let's Flip It" pins also became an important element of the campaign after many of their female interviewees told them they didn't wear caps. The PAR was critical to designing YADI's most long lasting youth-led campaign against horizontal violence.

Social Intervention Design

The next step after Design Research is getting down to designing our actual social intervention. At this point our design research has usually helped us hone in on an arrangement that we're interested in intervening in or a new one that we want to co-create with others. In addition to this, we may have found some ideas for a key element—an object, interaction or image that has symbolic meaning in the situation—that we can amplify through our intervention. We will look at how to do this through three intervention design techniques that DS4SI developed to better set the problem at the scale of arrangements and to craft effective social interventions at that scale:

Intervention Design Techniques

AMPLIFYING THE UNSPOKEN
A technique for Sensing Hidden Ideas and Arrangements

"THE SYMBOL AND THE THING"
A technique for Intervening in Arrangements

PRODUCTIVE FICTIONS
A technique for Imagining New Arrangements

Amplifying The Unspoken
A technique for Sensing Hidden Ideas and Arrangements

Much of everyday life and the ways we live it flow from unspoken and uninspected ideas and arrangements. When do we stop to wonder why there are outdoor basketball courts but not dance courts, or even how those basketball courts seem to have an invisible sign that says "boys only"? When do we ask how car culture created roads that are free, while subways and buses cost money? Or why the meta-arrangement of school has sorted children by exact age, rather than knowledge, interest or learning style?

If we are to create fundamental social change, we have to inspect deep-seated social ideas and the arrangements that flow from them. We need tactics that help populations unpack their assumptions about daily life and expose how the very same collective behaviors they are trying to change are embedded in these assumptions and arrangements. For example, players in our Space Bingo game (p. 68) were forced to look at the micro-spaces around them in new ways. What space had an identity crisis? What space was sanitized— and how? and by whom? Meanwhile, our "Is this chair one reason why...?" exercise (p. 72) helped educators explore the culpability of an overlooked everyday arrangement: the school chair as primary learning tool. Who did it serve? What ideas were embedded in it about good bodily behavior?

Another example of amplifying the unspoken was created by Barrington Edwards, a Boston-based artist and art teacher. In 2015 he used the media of sculpture and puppetry to get at the amplified, irrational fear of the black man. By creating a larger-than-life wearable black puppet, he represented how black men are always already seen as towering and therefore menacing. His character, Effingee, innocently roamed the streets of Boston interacting with young and old alike. Effingee amplified and made strange people's unspoken fear of black men, a fear that is most deadly to the feared themselves. As Barrington explains, "I approached this vexing social paradigm from the point of view of a satirist and storyteller. I intended for the piece to be layered and deep but cumbersome and ridiculous on the surface. I chose this tactic because of the absurdity of the reasoning that keeps coming up to rationalize the violence against the perceived threat of black men and boys." [20]

Artist Barrington Edward's Effingee character

By finding ways to amplify the unspoken, we can create the kinds of room necessary for people, communities and institutions to be re-arrangeable.

139

"The Symbol And The Thing"

A technique for Intervening in Arrangements

People, communities and cultures use symbols to make collective meaning, including agreements around desires and aversions, practices and taboos, and all sorts of ideas and arrangements. When Mayor Antanas Mockus intervened in the traffic life of Bogota by firing the traffic police and hiring over 400 mimes (p. 80), he was intervening in a symbol of government corruption and ineptitude. The traffic of Bogota—and the bribes it took to make your way through it—was an arrangement that every resident of Bogota was familiar with. As such, it was both a symbol and a real thing that Mockus could point to, play with or make strange.

KEEP IN MIND...

Moving and making are as important as talking and listening.

So much of our cultures of social change are driven by the spoken and written word. Social interventions often require working with other senses and actions: melting a gun, making a quilt, sharing an oversized gigantic book, or playing tug-of-war with total strangers could be the invitation into social transformation. This is another reason why it's so important to include artists and performers as we're designing interventions—to keep us aware of our sensorial habits and jostle us out of them!

When we talk about "the symbol and the thing", we are referring to when we can point to an arrangement—a gesture, item, infrastructure, habit, etc.—that operates on both the symbolic and literal levels. By being both a symbol and a real thing, it becomes something we can intervene in. Interventions like Lighting the Bridge (p. 86) functioned to intervene in specific arrangements that could then shift the larger issues of place-breaking. With Lighting the Bridge, a community could explore what was possible both

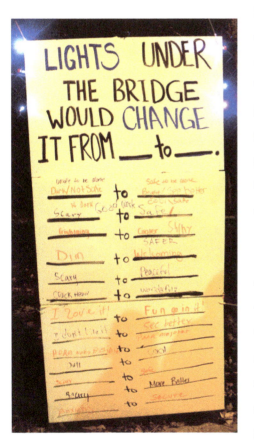

logistically and affectively when a dark, foreboding bridge underpass became brightly lit. We wanted the guerilla-style lighting of the bridge to seem so doable that passersby could start to think about what they would light—or build or paint or dance across—next.

Finding your key symbol will likely come during the discovery phase (p. 126). Whether you're doing user interviews, terrain observations, participatory action research or all of the above, keep your eyes and ears alert for something that could function as "the symbol and the thing."

It is useful to note that a symbol may be pulled from the context at play—like the dark bridge—or it may be pulled from another context, with the very unexpectedness of its usage serving as a powerful metaphor. For example, the AIDS Memorial Quilt began in 1985 when young AIDS activist Cleve Jones was inspired to use the symbol of the quilt to commemorate and make human the many people who died from AIDS. After helping hang a "patchwork" of posters with the names of AIDS victims, he recalls:

As I looked at that I thought it looked like some kind of odd quilt. And when I said the word quilt to myself, I thought of my grandma and great grandma, and it seemed like such a middle-American, traditional, family values sort of symbol. And I thought, what a perfect symbol to attach to this disease that's killing homosexuals and African Americans and IV drug users. So that was the idea. I could see how it would work as therapy for people who were grieving. I could see how it would work for the media to understand the lives behind the statistics, and as a weapon to shame the government for its inaction.[21]

Productive Fictions

A technique for Imagining New Arrangements

People tend to believe that arrangements are hard to change, and we don't disagree (although we would also argue that they are always changing). Our two previous design tools have gotten at the challenge of making complex arrangements—and the ideas embedded in them—more visible. This one gets at another challenge: that of our collective inability to imagine things being different. **We use what we call "productive fictions" to create glimpses into what might be in the world we want, and build micro-spaces where that world already exists.**

These productive fictions create room for people to jump off of our ideas and imagine new possibilities. For example, when activists and artists came to our Social Emergency Response Center (SERC, p. 94), they found themselves in a newly imagined and co-created infrastructure, with the metaphor of the emergency response center helping them move from addressing acute emergencies (like the state-induced crisis at the border) to "reconstructing democracy" with the understanding that only transformative rebuilding can keep the emergency from reoccurring. Inspired by the productive fiction, participants added their own elements to the SERC, from radical welcoming to interactive taiko drumming to a workshop on "writing your own manifesto."

The land of Wakanda (in the Black Panther comics and movie), was in essence a large scale productive fiction that gave us a glimpse into what an African nation could be like without colonization (p. 92). Its portrayal of such a country inspired people across the African diaspora. The power of productive fictions, then, is that once a sketch of a world is created, it gives its participants space to co-compose that world, from moviegoers spreading the Wakanda forever salute into one with meaning in everyday black life, to "blerds" (black nerds) creating black women coders' alliances inspired by the character of Princess Shuri (Black Panther's tech-wiz little sister), to activists co-composing spaces like Wakanda Dream Lab to blend Black Liberation and Afro-futurism.

Productive fictions make it possible for us to put flesh, experience and investment into co-composing the worlds we want. Through proposing a new arrangement with a set of underlying ideas, we get to co-create worlds that produce some of the effects we yearn for. It gives us a glimpse into our capacity to make social life, to make worlds. The invitation provided by a productive fiction becomes both a fantastical and practical exercise in making new worlds.

"[There is] the lack of imagination, the fear to imagine, the fear to imagine that there can be another reality for us…. Now what we do when we imagine is that within the prison of despair and fatalism, we throw an anchor and we start to pull ourselves towards this anchor. But by the very act of being able to throw something, to move, to generate a movement, we already declare that we remember how things could be. And we already acknowledge that there is a little bubble inside us, or around us, in which we are free. That we are not defined by the rigidity of the situation." [22]

- Israeli novelist David Grossman

KEEP IN MIND…

Avoid the temptation to make sure they "get it"!

Part of the power of great interventions is the space between the gesture and its public. If an insight is reached from the encounter, allow it to grow on its own. Give it room. Any attempt to "bring the point home" or reveal the moral of the story, as it were, turns what might be a transformative moment into what feels more like a lecture. We need to hold back from our urges to be literal ("do you get it?") and let people take what they do from the experience, more like it's a piece of art. Give it room.

Prototyping Social Interventions

To prototype means to test or model a new idea with the intention to make improvements. (We also use prototype as a noun, to point to the actual test or model that we're using to try out an idea.) Prototyping is an important part of design, as it gives us the mindset to be open, allow things to fail (or succeed in directions we hadn't imagined), and act to make adjustments accordingly. Too often folks who are trying to create change (at least from within the nonprofit sector) are not given this chance; we plan a large scale event or intervention, plan a new program or begin working with a new audience, all without getting to test our ideas and make improvements.

A prototype can range from physical and graphic mock-ups of a product, to play-testing a game, to practicing an intervention and seeing how your intended audience engages with it. We prototype to find out early on what might be inconsistent or getting in the way of a particular design's capacity for success. It's as much an inquiry into its style, aesthetics and communication system as it is into its ease of engagement or desired message. Good prototyping will help us solve some of the "clunkiness" of our interventions and get us to a simple, clear and elegant design.

Some of the things we prototype for include:

· Materials and functionality
· Style/Communication
· User Experience
· Gesture/Invitation
· Location/Scale/Timing

Prototyping For Functionality

We borrow the practice of prototyping from product design, where making physical models is the most common way to prototype. Specific types of models are used for testing different things. A *"works-like" model* tests for functionality, or how the model works for a particular group of people (what the design world calls "users"). For example, a works-like model of an electronic device might not have its final colors and materials chosen, but the placements of its buttons and how it feels to hold are all as accurate as possible, so that potential users can get a real sense of how it would—or wouldn't—work for them.

Example—Effingee

When artist Barrington Edwards was working on his giant man-puppet, Effingee (p. 139), he started by sketching his ideas for Effingee's looks and materials. Then he had to do quite a bit of materials testing to figure out what he could safely walk around in and what would convey the character he had created in his mind.

Prototyping For Style And Communication

A *looks-like model* offers a more accurate prototype of a particular product's aesthetics, in order to test things like attraction and communication. To quote Paul Watzlawick, author of *Pragmatics of Human Communication,* "One cannot not communicate." [23] Often when we are trying to create change, we communicate things that we are not aware of. Our styles—from our language to our clothes, font choices or product materials—may be communicating a personal preference or assumption, or an activist-aesthetic than attracts other activists but not necessarily our target audience. Prototyping our interventions with style and communication in mind makes it possible for potential users to interrogate our design choices and for us to make informed choices for how to proceed.

Example—Let's Flip It
When our participatory action researchers were working on Let's Flip It (p. 135), they were exploring how youth used baseball caps to nonverbally communicate the gangs, cliques or crews they were in. When trying to design a neutral cap, they first prototyped an all-black hat to symbolize all the colors together. This helped users point out to them that the black cap communicated some negative things that they hadn't intended. Another important thing that Let's Flip It prototyped was methods of delivery. To its youth designers, it was critical that youth got Let's Flip It materials (hats, stickers,

pins, etc.) from other young people; it was part of how they wanted to communicate that it was a youth-led solution. They prototyped a variety of methods, including a set of flyers with a Let's Flip It hotline that youth could call to get more Let's Flip It materials.

Respect the Magic Circle

KEEP IN MIND...

"All play moves and has its being within a play-ground marked off beforehand either materially or ideally, deliberately or as a matter of course....The arena, the card-table, the magic circle, the temple, the stage, the screen, the tennis court, the court of justice, etc., are all in form and function play-grounds, i.e., forbidden spots, isolated, hedged round, hallowed, within which special rules obtain. All are temporary worlds within the ordinary world, dedicated to the performance of an act apart." [24]

- From *Homo Ludens* by Johan Huizinga

Recognize what lengths we and others will go to if we're excited about the magic circle. We will play video games or surf social media for hours, pay hundreds of dollars to watch a play or sports event, or lose sleep while binge watching the latest must-see show. When we say, "Oh everyone's too busy," we may be inviting them into something that doesn't feel that magical! We can't disrespect the power of fun, play, and joy both in terms of being attractors and much needed creative generators in our work.

Prototyping For User Experience

When we think about prototyping social interventions, it is also critical that we test for user experience. Here there is much we can learn from game design. Game designers are in the business of creating engaging and compelling experiences, but they cannot tell their audience to have fun. They have to design a set of game rules and then prototype them to see if they are actually compelling for players. Our interventions are much like this: we are testing to see what an experience generates without being able to tell people what or how to feel about it. We also borrow from scenographers, set designers, and exhibit designers. We like how they pay attention to how scene setting and choreography have the power to create experience and mood.

Example—Public Kitchen
We knew we wanted to create an experience that would include ways for participants to both try out the Public Kitchen as an imagined infrastructure and add their ideas to it. Our first prototype was

 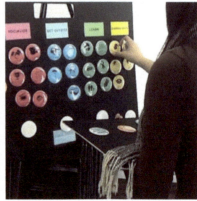

The Mobile Ideation Kit in action at Public Kitchen

somewhat of a mini-version: it was indoors and only for a day. That said, it included some of what ended up being core elements of the Public Kitchen (p. 98), like the recipe share and Mobile Ideation Kit.

Prototyping For Gesture/Invitation

Most of the time when we are designing social interventions, the intervention includes a gesture that amplifies the key symbol we've selected or some other invitation that connects it to its audience. It might be the elegant and humorous gesture of having mimes instead of traffic cops in Bogota (p. 80) or the invitation to share a meal at a Public Kitchen. At times the gesture is lost or the invitation falls flat. Sometimes the barrier for entry feels too high—someone is rushing for the bus and we're inviting them into an art project, say. Sometimes the invitation is too long-winded or complex. (We find that the initial "hook" has to be quite succinct and engaging!) Prototyping various gestures and invitations can help us realize that we may have nailed some part of our intervention and an adjustment on another part can help folks step in much more readily.

KEEP IN MIND...

How you show up is a part of your intervention.

Sometimes we forget that "our very bodies" are a part of our intervention. Who we are, what we bring in terms of history, affect, skills and style, are all a part of the overall intervention. We cannot look at our interventions without looking at ourselves.

Example—Tug of War

The first summer that we worked with youth to take on social violence, they ended up designing and playing "big urban games." They wanted to explore if they could use play to shift the affect created by the frequent violence in their neighborhoods. For their large scale version of tug-of-war, they played in the street: the walk signal was the sign to run out and begin the battle—stretching across a busy street with frantic excitement and effort. In this case the familiar game in a strange location functioned as both gesture and invitation. Passersby jumped in to help a side and drivers stopped to take pictures or play.

Prototyping For Logistics

Somewhat different from prototyping the core elements of our social intervention is prototyping the logistics of it, especially if we've designed it to be encountered in public space. Terrain research (p. 129) is critical here: Who is in the space, and when? Are people waiting for something or rushing by? Is it a different crowd on the weekend versus the weekdays? Sometimes we have to test sound, lighting, even police presence, depending on the intervention!

Example—The 50' Bench
The 50' Bench (p. 129) began when we installed a rough 6' prototype at a bus stop. When it consistently got used, it inspired Artist in Residence Claudia Paraschiv to co-create the magical "Seats of Power + Codex IV Corners" bench with local artists, residents, and passers-by. She also used plenty of other logistical prototyping, including when and where to have the outdoor building sessions, how to safely engage young children, etc.

Prototyping Process

Regardless of what we want our prototype to help us think about, we go through the same looping process to design and learn from our prototypes:

- Planning
- Testing in the field
- Reflection
- Iteration (begin again)

PLANNING

Before we go out in the field with our prototype, we spend time at the proverbial drawing board to plan it out and think about what we're trying to learn from it. For example, are we creating a "works-like" model or a "looks-like" model? Sometimes our prototypes can teach us multiple things (we might test for both physical functionality and location simultaneously), but it always helps to have a strong sense of what we want to learn from our prototype before we carry it out.

This planning phase also includes figuring out the logistics: who will 'deploy' the prototype, who will take notes or pictures, and when and where we are testing the prototype. (Sometimes multiple places and times help us learn what works best for the audience with whom we are trying to connect with.)

TESTING IN THE FIELD

This is usually the most nerve-wracking part of prototyping. We have to remind ourselves that our prototype is just a test, because sometimes it feels like people are calling our baby ugly! It's easy to get defensive or self-conscious when we're trying something new or strange in public. It's one of the most important reasons to prototype—this notion that how we show up is part of our intervention, and a part that can need practicing and testing, too.

Prototyping in the field is also a great time to learn things we don't expect. It may be about our prototype, or the space we're in, or the language we're using. It could be as simple as the time we realized that carrying clipboards made us look like we were doing surveys or asking for money (and trust us, folks ran the other way!). We try to keep an open mind and sharp senses to capture the unexpected and adjust in real time.

REFLECTION

First we give ourselves time to process our emotions—"Oh my god, it worked! They loved it! We're awesome!" or "That was really awkward! It didn't go at all like we hoped. It sucks." Then we try to dig into what we can learn from our experience in the field. We ask ourselves questions beyond if it "worked" or not, and get to what we were testing for and what we saw/heard/felt while in action. We use our Design Research Questions (p. 159) to consider what ideas, arrangements and effects the prototype might have impacted.

ITERATION

Based on our reflections and what we learned from our prototype, we begin the loop again: going back to the drawing board to plan how our new insights will impact our social intervention design. This process does not have to starkly differentiate our prototypes from our "final" intervention either. Many of our interventions have ended up being prototypes in their own right, like when a Public Kitchen or SERC pops up in new places, based on our early interventions.

Prototyping our interventions is very much part of the process of designing them, but it also flows into our next challenge: how we evaluate our social interventions across ideas, arrangements and effects.

Evaluating Social Interventions

"Did it work?"

Typically the question "Did it work?" is asked from within the same conceptual habits of thought that separate effects from ideas and arrangements in the first place. It only wonders about effects: "When we did this, did it decrease X (negative effect) or increase Y (positive effect)?" We always hope to, but since effects are created by multiple overlapping and sturdy arrangements and ideas, looking at effectiveness strictly within the realm of effects can be misleading. It might look like we failed because we didn't immediately change an effect, when we actually laid the groundwork for a powerful new arrangement. Conversely, it might look like we succeeded because we saw incremental improvement in an effect, but if we are not changing arrangements or ideas, that success might be short lived. We need to be able to differentiate a social intervention that just isn't effective (that happens too!) from one that might be creating a wide variety of interesting outcomes, even if it doesn't measure up to a traditional take on "Did it work?"

We believe social interventions should be evaluated across the I-A-E framework, rather than just in regards to effects. Here are some questions that help us do that.

I-A-E Questions for Evaluating Social Interventions

IDEAS

What new line of possibility does this intervention point out?

How does this intervention help us think better about a problem or desire?

How does it help us think differently about a place, population, arrangement or issue?

How does it challenge existing ideas, stereotypes or stigmas?

How does it help us understand what we want to start vs. what we want to stop?

What does it inspire and what does it make us want to better understand?

How does this intervention invite people into thinking in new ways?

How does it help people both generate and share new ideas?

ARRANGEMENTS

How does this intervention help us see hidden or overlapping arrangements?

How does it help people question or think differently about arrangements that we take for granted?

How does it help people come up with new ideas for intervening in arrangements?

How does it help us imagine and/or test new arrangements?

What does it inspire us to re-arrange in our everyday lives?

EFFECTS

How does this intervention help unearth effects that we are not paying attention to?

How does it generate effects—intended or unintended—that we are interested in?

How does it have ephemeral effects, like changing an atmosphere in a space?

How does it create a transformative or irreversible change in effects?

The Other Question: "Did it fail?

"Did it fail?" is a fairly unbearable question, mostly because far too often we hear it as "Did I fail?" As humans, we often become emotionally attached to the interventions we try, such that we can't see it if they're not working. We become defensive, narrow-visioned, and nose-to-the-grindstone, thinking either "I'll show them," or "If I just try harder this will work." Sometimes we have to be open to the fact that we may be on the wrong path, or at a false maxima (where we think we're at the peak, but really it's just a little hill, and if we could look around, we might see a much higher peak).

An easier question to handle might be: "What didn't work?" It goes well with its partner, "What did work?", and between the two questions, we might get where we need to go in terms of evaluating our intervention. When we are looking at both what did and didn't work, we need to go back into the discovery (or research) phase, because essentially we are beginning an informed redesign of our intervention. This often includes more user research, terrain research and conceptual research (p. 127). Here are some questions that we find useful.

Design Research Questions for Evaluating Social Interventions

USER RESEARCH

Did the people who you wanted to experience the intervention actually experience it?

If so, what were their responses? (Did they engage with it? Avoid it? Share it with others? etc.)

Did you have unanticipated users? If so, what were their responses?

What did the intervention shift—if anything—in terms of how the intended users were experiencing the problem you were trying to address?

TERRAIN RESEARCH

How did the intervention affect the space?

Did it shift who was at the center and who was at the margins of the space?

Did it shift how people saw the space or felt in the space?

Did it change any formal or informal rules about the space?

Are there ways you might have gotten the space wrong—were you in the wrong space, or in the right space at the wrong time?

CONCEPTUAL RESEARCH

The questions about ideas, arrangements and effects from "Did it work?" (p. 157) are great questions for getting at this conceptual research; ie— Did your intervention change ideas? (Did it bring about new awareness about arrangements? etc.)

PARTICIPATORY ACTION RESEARCH

As we said in the PAR section (p. 135), engaging a PAR team throughout your social intervention design and execution is ideal. This team can then join you for the three research types above.

Changing the prescription or upping the dosage?

Sometimes we are so sure that what we are doing is right, our only goal seems to be upping the dosage. "Can we reach more people?" "Can this be a model program?" Frequently, we base our enthusiasm on our love for our intervention, as well as on evaluation into why and how our intervention is working for those it is.

But what about those it's not working for? Upping the dosage can cause sickness! We need to be open to changing the prescription sometimes too. (And looking for, and listening to, the folks who aren't involved in our successful interventions.)

Intervention is always risky.

We must remember this for a few reasons. Sometimes we default to what we know works (to some degree…), what we know is fundable, or what we know doesn't seem too out of place. Usually the more we default to this, the farther we are getting from effective intervention. These are crazy times, and they require some crazy sounding interventions! Additionally, as we check in with ourselves about our own psychic ability to take risks, to act silly in the face of desperate times, to risk people's anger or our own well-being, we must also take care of ourselves, give ourselves permission to fail, to play, to rest, and to eat!

In closing, it's important to keep in mind that we still practice in a world whose habits and discourses function from a standpoint that changing effects qua effects is what matters most. Oftentimes this is because negative effects are extremely urgent—state-sanctioned violence against the black community, effects of climate change, sexual violence, etc. This urgency can cause us to default to focusing on the effect as the thing to change, versus focusing on the effect as being a way into, an indicator of a more complex set of arrangements out of which the effects emerge.

Even when we fight an effect as a way to address a larger idea—fighting police violence or education inequality as a way to fight racism—the effects often consume us. When we're stuck looking for solutions within the realm of changing effects, we can get mired in quasi-solutions like police body cameras or smaller class sizes; these are not to be overlooked, but don't get us to challenging the larger arrangements of policing or even schools. In their limitations, they keep those of us who care deeply about social justice too busy fighting over effects to get to the work of imagining profound new arrangements of justice or education.

Here is where design comes in. The designerly approach of curiosity and experimentation can help us see our way from the problem (or negative effects) into a more complex set of arrangements. Bringing together multiple kinds of thinkers can challenge us to make sense of the problem in a new way or even reframe it altogether. Designing social interventions can invite the greater public into questioning some of the arrangements at play, or co-composing entirely new ones that could generate solutions that we wouldn't have imagined ourselves.

CONCLUSION

*All politics, including revolutionary political action, will succeed
only if it is canny about deploying multiple forms. Revolutions
must mobilize certain arrangements, certain organized forms
of resistance—the takeover of the public square, the strike, the
boycott, the coalition....Which forms do we wish to see governing
social life, then, and which forms of protest or resistance actually
succeed at dismantling unjust, entrenched arrangements?* [25]

- Caroline Levine, *Forms: Whole, Rhythm, Hierarchy, Network*

We believe rearranging the social is a practical and powerful way to
"dismantle unjust, entrenched arrangements" and imagine vibrant
new ones. The I-A-E framework begins this work by deepening our
understanding of the social contexts we hope to change and improve,
as well as expanding our capacity for designing the world we truly
want. It flows from our premise that *ideas are embedded in social
arrangements, which in turn produce effects.*

For folks who care about social justice, it is hard not to get caught
up in the constant struggle of fighting negative effects—they come
at us so fast and furiously. We can almost get whiplash moving from
school closings to school shootings, from immigrants locked up at
our border to black and brown people locked up in our prisons, from
climate catastrophes to the mistreatment of poor people hardest

hit by them. Even when we can point to the big ideas behind these effects—racism, capitalism, xenophobia, sexism, etc.—we can be stymied by their sturdiness and trickiness. At DS4SI, we trace this sturdiness to the many ways that these ideas are entrenched in daily arrangements—from the physical arrangements of chairs, cities or borders to the social arrangements of interactions, expectations, or hierarchies. For this reason, we consider these uninspected daily arrangements a rich and undertapped terrain for social change.

If we are to rearrange the social, we must hone our abilities to sense, intervene in and re-imagine these existing social arrangements of daily life. We do so through social intervention. Not only can social interventions help us do the critical work of making arrangements changeable, but they can function as powerful invitations for others to join us. An effective social intervention might suddenly make an existing arrangement seem strange enough for its users to question the ideas embedded in it. Or it might create a new arrangement with just enough flavor to engage its users in co-composing it, and in so doing, generating new ideas about themselves and each other.

We are making the case that social interventions as an approach to social justice can work alongside traditional approaches—community organizing, unions, electoral politics, mass movements—as a way to engage our communities in designing, re-imagining and fundamentally changing our lives. We see changing social arrangements as a fundamental lever for achieving social justice. We do not mean some sort of trick lever that by-passes conflict or struggle. In fact, this won't be easy at all. Attempting to rearrange social life goes against the power of existing arrangements and all those who benefit from such arrangements. It also demands that we take on ourselves. We are as much a product of the already arranged as anything or anyone else. In fact we are entangled in arrangements sensorially, emotionally and relationally. So we must confront how we collude with the forces of power that we are up against, even as we go up against them.

Currently, arrangements of power and authority (and even media and daily life) are conglomerating at unprecedented rates, necessitating that we find new arrangements for confronting such power. To us this means developing our skills at engaging a greater public, believing that as we create opportunities for people to explore, experience and design the future they want, it will increase our power and numbers to fight for that future. As we test these new possible arrangements, they themselves can give us new ideas for how we build and confront power. And as we dig into not just changing effects but challenging arrangements and ideas, we can create new possibilities and invitations for collective transformation.

In this way, rearranging the social is imperative if we want to bring our ideas about justice beyond our silos—activism, art, education, planning, law, etc.—and into the daily lives of millions of people.

It demands that our strategies for social justice become, well, more social. It requires that we see ourselves as designers of everyday life: as interested in what's possible in our public spaces or weekend plans as we are in what policy is about to pass or fail. When we think with the audacity of world builders, we begin to see not just new ways of fighting for a more just and vibrant society, but whole new ideas about what that world might be like.

AFTERWORD

By Mindy Thompson Fullilove

When I was a psychiatric resident, I saw a video of the therapy of a young woman who was recovering from drug addiction. The meeting included the patient, the grandmother with whom she was living, and the therapist. At the beginning of the session, the three were spaced equally apart. As the conversation went on, and the difficulties the grandmother was experiencing in managing her granddaughter became clear, the therapist picked up her chair and moved it beside the grandmother's. There was a shift in the room after that. Suddenly, the grandmother started to act as if she had the right to set limits and the granddaughter started to listen to her with respect. I was shocked to see this, and wanted to learn "moving chairs therapy." I am still on that kick forty years later, which is perhaps why the Design Studio for Social Intervention asked me to write this afterword. I know that we can change arrangements with surprising outcomes for effects and ideas.

I have seen many changes in arrangements. In the early of years of the AIDS epidemic, the public health community focused on the problems of individual risk behaviors. When I asked about the structures creating risk, I was told, "You can't change structure." As the Reagan presidency was very busy changing structure to concentrate wealth and disempower the poor, I realized that what they were saying was, "Mindy, *you* can't change structure."

About that time, I learned of a public policy called planned shrinkage which had closed fire stations in poor neighborhoods in New York City. That massive change in the arrangement of fire protection services precipitated a fire epidemic that ravaged poor minority neighborhoods. Drs. Deborah and Rodrick Wallace have documented the dire effects that followed change in the arrangement: loss of housing, spread of the AIDS epidemic, increase in violence, drug addiction and infant and maternal mortality.

By contrast, I have seen the life-affirming urbanism of Michel Cantal-Dupart, who demonstrated the ways in which changing arrangements could reanimate a stagnant neighborhood, bringing a city back to life. His work in Perpignan, France, for example, re-arranged the streets so that a marginalized neighborhood had easy access to downtown. He followed that by moving a fenced-in soccer field from the middle of the neighborhood, where it was blocking people's movement. He moved the field to a more peripheral space that needed the comings and goings of athletic youth. In the middle of the neighborhood, he inserted a gracious and welcoming park that stimulated people's comings and goings.

Having seen all this, I know what these tools of ideas-arrangements-effects can do for us, as we face this dire moment of climate change, tyranny, mass extinction and international war, on the global scale, and poverty, housing shortages, and stagnant wages at home. We need tools that we can use to address these problems, and it can't be just the same old tools we've been using all along. This is where this excellent guide to ideas-arrangements-effects comes in. We can start at any point, by identifying ideas we need to update, arrangements that might be altered for the better and effects that we propose to more in better directions. We need to keep in mind that no problem is localized to a place or a group of people. By thinking across scales, we will be able to take advantage of the reverberations that echo across dimensions. Teenagers who stop grilling one another might start grilling elected officials about moving on climate change for example.

We don't know what the limits are for these moves. We do know we have no time to waste if we want to make a better future for all. My father, Ernest Thompson, was a union and community organizer who wrote about his experiences in

Homeboy Came to Orange: A Story of People's Power. He closed his book on this note of urgency, saying:

The United States is at the crossroads. And time has run out. It has run out on us morally in the eyes of humankind and in the eyes of God. We have no more time for war, or exploitation, or poisoning the earth. We must learn to live together now. The problem in the United States of people living together is a Black-white problem. The separatists— be they Black or white—only obstruct our way. They have no answers for the tasks confronting us. These tasks are too crucial to be entrusted to the warmongers and the profiteers. The money-changers must once again be driven from the temple so that the people can prevail, for only the people can be entrusted with their own future.

We *can* change structure. Let's do it.

Mindy Thompson Fullilove, MD, LFAPA, HonAIA
Author of Root Shock: How Tearing Up City Neighborhoods Hurts America, and What We Can Do About It

ACKNOWLEDGMENTS

This book comes out of over a decade of practice. That practice was very new for us when we started, and we took a lot of chances and wrong turns as we decided to develop an approach to design for the social justice sector. And though we were pretty well versed in methodology development, this was still a bold endeavor. It took brave leadership from many early adapters and allies for us to get to where we are now in terms of understanding our approach and the framework of IAE.

Ceasar McDowell gave us a fellowship at the Center for Reflective Community Practice within MIT's Department of Urban Studies and Planning that really started this entire journey. It was there that we met Rob Peagler, who co-founded DS4SI with us before moving back into more traditional design work. Our love for "the magic circle," our notion of cloaked co-conspirators and our search for new forms started in conversations with Rob.

Some of our earliest testing of interventions occurred in partnership with Project South when they hosted the first United States Social Forum (USSF) in 2007. They continue to believe in us and improve our work, and we are deeply grateful.

We want to thank Boston-area youth organizing groups like BYOP, The City School, DSNI, Project Hip Hop and others (with special thanks to thought partner Najma Nazy'at), for being the first set of groups that asked us to work with them. We got to do some of our earliest and most interesting work in those days. Many thanks to the young people who were willing to take risks and try new approaches for addressing social violence.

Many thanks to Judith Leemann, the brilliant artist and thinker who introduced the power of metaphoric thinking at that time, who was our first artist-in-residence, and who continues to push our thinking in new directions.

Kiara Nagel, Vicky Takamine, and Albino Garcia, Jr. laid the groundwork in our cultural commons project for what would later show up in Public Kitchen, The Public: a Work in Progress and our Spatial Justice paper. Thanks for working with us in those early days when we were still figuring out our techniques and processes.

Ditra Edwards and Makani Themba of the Praxis Project were also pivotal for us getting to this stage. They made us part of their national capacity building team for CCHE (Communities Creating Healthy Environments) when we were still a very young organization. It was at their Roots & Remedies Conferences that we ran our first creativity labs, which became one of the primary practices of the Studio.

We owe so many thanks to a variety of on-going collaborators and thought partners, including Alvaro Lima, Dudley Street Neighborhood Initiative (DSNI), Ena Fox, our Fairmount Cultural Corridor partners, Hampshire College, Karlos Schmeider and the SouthWest Organizing Project (SWOP), Liam VanVleet, MassArt's Center for Art & Community Practice (CACP), National Education Association, SenseLab, Tufara Muhammad, the University of Orange, and more.

All of our direct intervention work has been in partnership with artists and activists. We are so grateful for the skills, knowledge and relationships that they brought to our work, from co-creating SERCs to co-designing big urban games, to building mobile kitchens, to lighting bridges, to interactive taiko drumming and so much more. And much appreciation to all the willing participants who bravely and curiously stepped into strange new arrangements and social interventions. Without them, none of this would be possible!

Third Sector New England (now TSNE MissionWorks) took a chance on us when we had only one grant to our name, and we are grateful they've stuck with us as our fiscal sponsor. Special thanks to Lisa Tobias and Svenja Oberender who constantly translated those muggle arrangements to us!

Speaking of grants, our work has rarely fit into neat boxes, so we are grateful to the funders and program officers who believed in it and managed to fund it anyway, including ArtPlace America, Barr Foundation, The Boston Foundation, Ford Foundation, Hyams Foundation, Kellogg Foundation, Kresge Foundation, New England

Foundation for the Arts, New World Foundation, Open Society Foundation, Robert Wood Johnson Foundation, and Surdna Foundation. And special thanks to program officers F. Javier Torres, Klare Shaw and Patricia Jerido for their belief in the Studio's approach.

We've made lots of friends and allies along the way. We'd like to thank everyone who has thought with us, attended our events, and walked with us along the journey. They are too many to mention individually, but each one of them has helped enormously.

Thanks to Arturo Escobar and Mindy Fullilove for your kind words on both ends of the book and the many ways you've furthered our thinking about arrangements. Thanks Matthew Hern for your coaching and helping us get the book from concept to reality.

Special thanks to Walter Santory who generously taught Summitt, our Executive Dog, about the arrangement of lunch.

NOTES

1   *Oxford Poverty & Human Development Initiative (OPHI).* Oxford
     Department of International Development, ophi.org.uk/policy/
     national-policy/gross-national-happiness-index/.

2   Warren-Findlow, Jan. "Weathering: Stress and Heart Disease in
     African American Women Living in Chicago." Qualitative Health
     Research, vol. 16, no. 2, Feb. 2006.

3   Hacking, Ian. "Making Up People." *London Review of Books*, vol.
     28, no. 16, 17 Aug. 2006, www.lrb.co.uk/v28/n16/ian-hacking/
     making-up-people.

4   Sharpe, Christina. *In the Wake: On Blackness and Being.* Durham,
     Duke University Press, 2016.

5   Eubanks, Virginia. "I'm often asked 'Aren't tools neutral?...'"
     Twitter, 24 Oct. 2018, twitter.com/PopTechWorks/
     status/1055142107458007040.

6   Rennis, Lesley Green, et al. "'We Have a Situation Here' Using
     Situational Analysis for Health and Social Research." *Qualitative
     Research in Social Work,* edited by Anne E. Fortune et al., Second
     ed., New York City, Columbia University Press, 2013.

7   Alexander, Michelle. "We Are Not the Resistance." New York Times
     [New York City], 21 Sept. 2018, Opinion sec., www.nytimes.
     com/2018/09/21/opinion/sunday/ resistance-kavanaugh-trump-
     protest.html.

8   Lambert, Steve. "Creative Time Summit 2012: Tactics–Steve
     Lambert." 12 Oct. 2012. *Creative Time,* creativetime.org/
     summit/2012/10/12/steve-lambert/. Speech.

9   Lobenstine, Lori, and Bailey, Kenneth. "Redlining the Adjacent Possible: Youth and Communities of Color Face the (Not) New Future of (Not) Work." 29 Dec. 2015. *Open Society Foundations,* static.opensocietyfoundations.org/misc/ future-of-work/the-informal-economy-and-the-evolving-hustle.pdf. Working paper.

10   Douglas, Mary. *Purity and Danger: an Analysis of Concepts of Pollution and Taboo.* ARK ed., New York City, Routledge, 1984.

11   "Bogotá Improving Civic Behavior Cities on Speed." *YouTube,* uploaded by Eduardo Lopez, 13 Apr. 2014, www.youtube.com/ watch?v=4lOkLNIT3gI.

12   Lobenstine, Lori, and Bailey, Kenneth. "Notes from the Field: Design Studio for Social Intervention." *International Journal of Qualitative Studies in Education*, vol. 32, no. 10, Nov. 2019.

13   Highmore, Ben. *Everyday Life and Cultural Theory.* London, Routledge, 2002.

14   Simon, Herbert. *The Sciences of the Artificial.* Cambridge, The MIT Press, 1969.

15   Manzini, Ezio. *Design, When Everybody Designs: An Introduction to Social Innovation.* Cambridge, The MIT Press, 2015.

16   Flemons, Douglas. *Completing Distinctions: Interweaving the Ideas of Gregory Bateson and Taoism into a Unique Approach to Therapy.* Boston, Shambhala Publications, 1991.

17   Heaton, John. "Laing and Psychotherapy." *R D Laing Contemporary Perspectives*, edited by Salman Raschid, London, Free Association Books, 2005.

18   Salen, Katie, and Zimmerman, Eric. *Rules of Play*. Cambridge, The MIT Press, 2004.

19   Borda, O.F.. "Investigating reality in order to transform it: The Colombian experience." *Dialectical Anthropology*, vol. 4, no. 1, 1979.

20   Lobenstine, Lori, and Bailey, Kenneth. "Cultural Tactics." 13 July 2016. DS4SI, www.ds4si.org/writings/2016/7/13/cultural-tactics. Working paper.

21   "Cleve Jones on Harvey Milk & AIDS Memorial Quilt." *YouTube*, uploaded by Xtra: Canada's Gay & Lesbian News, 29 Nov. 2011, www. youtube.com/ watch?v=fEObIgSXtBY

22   Grossman, David. "David Grossman has become the first Israeli author to win the Man Booker International Prize." *BBC Newshour*, BBC, 15 June 2017. Interview.

23   Watzlawick, Paul, Bavelas, Janet Beavin, and Jackson, Don D. *Pragmatics of Human Communication*. New York City, W.W. Norton and Company, Inc, 2011.

24   Huizinga, Johan. *Homo Ludens: A Study of the Play-Element in Culture*. Kettering, Angelico Press, 2016.

25   Levine, Caroline. *Forms: Whole, Rhythm, Hierarchy, Network*. Princeton, Princeton University Press, 2017.

PHOTO AND ARTIST CREDIT

The vast majority of the photos in this book were taken by DS4SI, or by artists and participants who shared their photos with us. Here are some specific contributions by photographers and partnering artists:

Page 35
Mobile Kitchen design and photography by Golden Arrows.

Pages 94-97
Boston SERC photography by Anselmo Cassiano, Joanna Tam, Nabil Vega. Additional SERCs photographed include SERC Houston at Project Row Houses (commissioned artists Tiago Gualberto and Maria Molteni), SERC at PolicyLink Chicago, SERC at Digaaí Boston (led by Alvaro Lima), SERC Utica (led by Datule Artist Collective and Mississippi Center for Cultural Production), MassArt SERCs (led by students in the Center for Art and Community Partnerships).

Pages 98-101, 150
Public Kitchen photography by Kelly Creedon, Travis Watson, Golden Arrows and DS4SI.

Original Public Kitchen included commissioned artists Golden Arrows and Nadine Nelson.

Page 139
Effingee photograph by Aziza Robinson-Goodnight.

External Photo Credits

Page 27
Russell, Lee. *Oklahoma City streetcar terminal*. 1939. *Wikimedia Commons*.

Page 66
"Capitalism Works for Me!" installation by Steve Lambert. Photo courtesy of the artist.

Page 70
Lobenstine, Lori, and Bailey, Kenneth. "Redlining the Adjacent Possible: Youth and Communities of Color Face the (Not) New Future of (Not) Work." 29 Dec. 2015. DS4SI, www.ds4si.org/ writings/2015/12/29/ redlining-the-adjacent-possible-youth-and-communities-of-color-face-the-not-new-future-of-not-work. Working paper. (Photo credits p12-13.)

Page 81
El Tiempo. Traffic mime. *The Harvard Gazette,* news.harvard.edu/gazette/ story/ 2004/03/academic-turns-city-into-a-social-experiment/.

Page 92
Loika, Pat. Cosplay of Black Panther, DragonCon 2013. 1 Sept. 2013. *Wikimedia Commons,* commons.wikimedia.org/wiki/File:Dragon_Con_2013_-_Wakanda_(9697954480).jpg.

ds4si

The Design Studio for Social Intervention is dedicated to changing how social justice is imagined, developed and deployed in the United States. Situated at the intersections of design practice, social justice, public art, and popular engagement, DS4SI designs and tests social interventions with and on behalf of marginalized populations, controversies and ways of life. Founded in 2005 and based in Boston, DS4SI is a space where activists, artists, academics and the larger public come together to imagine new approaches to social change and new solutions to complex social issues.